Testimonials for
Embodied Everyday Awakening

"Geri Portnoy's *Embodied Everyday Awakening* is a brilliant guiding light, demonstrating how challenges are catalysts for a new level of consciousness. It offers hope that spiritual awakening can lead us to a brighter, more compassionate future."

—**Betsey Downing,** PhD,
climate educator, yoga and meditation teacher

"In *Embodied Everyday Awakening,* Geri Portnoy shares from her own experience of awakening to offer a guidebook that reveals how the very ordinary moments of our everyday life can become vehicles for expanding awareness."

—**Jeff Carreira,**
author of *The Soul's Journey to Wholeness*

"In this book, Geri Portnoy addresses the crisis of disconnection and loneliness and offers a process to help us awaken to a new level of consciousness. Unlike past paradigms, this modern-day awakening is not an escape from our woes but a full immersion into a new way of life."

—**Desiree Rumbaugh,**
international yoga teacher

"This book is authentic, relatable, practical, and full of wisdom, love, and real-life examples that activate and expand your awakening."

—Eileen Hahn,
leadership consultant,
author of *The Job You Were Born For*

EMBODIED EVERYDAY AWAKENING

*A guide to spiritual transformation
in the midst of daily life*

GERI PORTNOY

Embodied Everyday Awakening:
A guide to spiritual transformation in the midst of daily life

Geri Portnoy

Published by Yoga of Awakening

Yoga of Awakening

Limit of Liability/Disclaimer of Warranty:

Publishing and editorial team: Author Bridge Media,
www.AuthorBridgeMedia.com
Editor: Helen Chang
Publishing Manager: Laurie Aranda

Library of Congress Control Number: 2025920116

ISBN: – softcover: 979-8-9863484-0-7
ISBN: – hardcover: 979-8-9863484-2-1
ISBN: – ebook: 979-8-9863484-1-4

Ordering Information:

Quantity sales. Special discounts are available on quantity purchases by corporations, associations, and others. For details, contact the publisher at the address above.

DEDICATION

I dedicate this book to you, the reader.

*May this book support your awakening and
the awakening of our world.*

CONTENTS

ACKNOWLEDGMENTS

I did not write this book alone. It took a village of people to support and believe in me, and I am deeply grateful to each of you.

I want to extend my heartfelt thanks to Author Bridge Media for listening to my vision and helping me transform it into a reality. Helen Chang, your skill in structuring the story has given voice to the incredible journey of awakening. Laurie Aranda, my project manager, your encouragement and creativity have been instrumental in bringing this book into the world. Denise Cassino, I'm so grateful for your support in the launch of this book.

Special thanks to my yoga teachers, Lee Ann Carey, Tim Miller, John Friend, Desiree Rumbaugh, and Betsey Downing, whose yogic wisdom inspired my journey of spiritual awakening.

A deep bow of appreciation to my spiritual awakening teachers, including Lloyd Francis, Greg Aurand, Saniel and Linda Bonder, Rod Taylor, Ted Strauss, Deborah Boyar, Adam Chacksfield, Adyashanti, Judith Blackstone, Jeff Foster, Eckhart Tolle, Patricia Albere, Jeff Carreira, Loch Kelly, and Thomas Hübl. Thank you for showing me that awakening is possible through your living example and for providing guidance, tools, practices, and transmission to help catalyze my awakening.

I am deeply grateful to all the students who have shared their stories of transformation in my awakening groups over the years. Your bravery and generosity have enriched this book. I am incredibly thankful to those who allowed their stories to be shared here in the pages of this book. Thank you for inspiring others with your courageous, beautiful journey.

To those who contributed funding to launch this project. Thank you for your generosity and belief in the power of awakening.

Thanks to my family for encouraging me to live fully.

Finally, special thanks to my beloved partner, Kevin, for your inspiration, love, and support.

OPENING

There is only one time when it is essential to awaken. That time is now.—Jack Kornfield

Evolving Within

Do you ever feel overwhelmed or exhausted? Are you sometimes struck with a sense of despair or grief—the knowledge that something is wrong, but you can't quite define what? Do the things that used to give you joy lack the meaning they once had?

Do you feel like there's something wrong with you, or life, or with other people? Or do you have an inner discomfort or dissatisfaction, even though you have all or most of the material things you want?

Do you feel a longing for something more and experience grief that you aren't where you want to be? Do you think: "I should be happier," or "I should be more grateful." All you have to do is be more positive, right? You drink an extra cup of coffee, push yourself harder, and accomplish more. You push the feelings down, carry on. Yet you feel a greater and greater sense of exhaustion, despair, or hopelessness. And you keep coming back to that grief, that striving, and you're uncertain about what to do next.

If you identified with any of the above, you're not alone. Your old ways may have stopped working, and a new way has yet to emerge. You are in the in-between, liminal space of the unknown. You may be ready for the next stage of your life—your awakening process—the next natural stage of your transformational journey.

My intention with this book is to provide a guiding hand to help you move through this journey. You may be completely new to spiritual awakening. You may be a successful person in life, but you haven't had time to pay deep attention or listen to your inner world. Or you may already have a spiritual practice. You may do yoga, or meditation, and it may have been part of your life for many years.

Whatever your experiences, this book can be useful for you. No matter where you're starting, you're here because you are feeling some gnawing sense of dissatisfaction with your life right now. You may sense that there's something more, you may be hungry to experience a deeper connection with yourself and other people, or perhaps you long to feel the sacredness of life.

The unknown reality is you are a divine human being, and it's your birthright to *spiritually awaken*—to wake up and know Who You Are.

Awakening to the Spirit

Embodied spiritual awakening is the process of connecting with Fundamental Consciousness: the part of us that is interconnected to everyone and everything. Modern-day awakening unfolds *throughout* your everyday life. You don't have to—and shouldn't!—step outside of your family, workplace, culture, or body to awaken. Instead, you can awaken in the midst of your everyday life.

As you awaken, you feel the discomfort of living with outdated habits, patterns, and conditioning. Noticing your own dissatisfaction is a sign of your readiness for spiritual awakening. Through awakening, you learn to befriend yourself, to stop the war within. We often have an idea of negative (uncomfortable) and positive (comfortable) emotions, but both are natural parts of our wholeness. As you awaken, you learn to embrace and acknowledge every part of yourself. The awakening journey helps you reclaim the wholeness of your humanity, while also unveiling your divinity as Fundamental Consciousness—intimately connected to all of life. Awakening brings you into service to a larger unfolding of life.

Once you connect to the innate well-being of Fundamental Consciousness, you will feel supported and held. You will be able to let go of the habitual striving, forcing, and struggling people often experience in the first part of their lives. Instead, you will be able to relax and surrender into the natural flow of your own awakened being.

From this awakened state, you can relax into life and be more of your whole self. Instead of longing, you will feel an innate sense of fulfillment. You will have the space to be more vulnerable and more authentic, because your okayness is sourced from your inner world and interconnectedness of being, not from the reactions of other people.

Journeying Together

I am so pleased to be able to be your guide on this journey. I wish I had started my journey with this book, so I would have had a clearer understanding of how to cooperate with my own awakening process, had been able to judge myself less along the way, and could have surrendered to the process more easily.

I have been on the spiritual path since the mid 1980s, reading and engaging in various practices, including yoga and meditation. In 1999, I founded a yoga studio so I could share these transformational practices with others. I devoted myself to my own spiritual awakening journey in 2004, and several years later I had a profound awakening shift. It was an amazing transformation that changed my life forever. Almost immediately I understood that this was my purpose in life: to share embodied awakening with people who were hungry to wake up and know who they are.

In 2009, I became a spiritual awakening coach, forming

awakening groups to help students transition smoothly into their embodied spiritual awakening. Since then, I've worked with hundreds of people, supporting and guiding their journey of awakening.

In this book I share some of their amazing stories. It is a guide that offers instructions, practices, perspectives, and insights to help facilitate your transformational journey. Your everyday life is the sacred ground for unfolding your transformational journey, and the path begins right here.

Chapter 1

INITIATION

The awakening of consciousness is the next evolutionary step for mankind.—Eckhart Tolle

Exploring the Crisis

Most of us can agree that society has reached a crisis point. We can see it in the devastation we are causing the earth, the unsustainability of the mechanisms of society, and the collapse of political cooperation as we fail to work with each other as interconnected beings. We're reaching a place, individually and collectively, where the old way is no longer working.

Although this may be difficult, it isn't entirely negative. It's an invitation to evolve from the first stage of our lives and enter into the second stage of life—the journey of awakening. The challenge lies in the fact that most of us simply don't know how to grow into this next phase.

I believe humanity is moving into the next era—the *spiritual awakening* era. We are in the midst of a spiritual awakening personally, culturally, and globally. The old, outdated ways are breaking down, and the new ways are not always apparent. What's next is a movement that will include what's been excluded—to welcome our emotions, body sensations, and spiritual nature. It is time to unfold a whole new level of living, both from our divinity and our evolved humanity. We're ready for the next stage of life. We're ready for spiritual awakening.

Entering the Second Stage of Adult Life

Just because we're ready, though, doesn't mean we know how to take the first step.

There's a metaphoric story that comes from recovery circles:

When humans first started making long sea voyages, a lot of people would get sick and die. No one could figure out why—it seemed to strike at random and could take entire ships down with it. People were sick, and they knew it, but they didn't know what was missing. It wasn't until James Lind discovered that citrus fruit stopped the mystery disease that people realized the importance of Vitamin C. Ships started to carry limes on board, and sailors stopped dying of scurvy.

Modern society faces a similar crisis. We are spiritually sick. Our young people are dying of suicide at an unprecedented rate, our society's love for guns is leading to horrifying violence, and levels of depression and anxiety are beyond what we've seen in the past. We can see the effects, but most people have no idea what's causing it. I believe we as human beings are missing an essential nutrient: our spiritual vitamin C. We've lost the connection with our essential spiritual nature and fundamental well-being.

That's why I started guiding individuals in their embodied spiritual awakening journey. Through individual coaching and small group interactions, individuals are able to drop more into their bodies. This helps them reconnect to themselves and wake up to Fundamental Consciousness. They find that missing part of themselves and answer the question, "Who am I?" Relieved, they finally feel, "Oh, I'm home." They relax and release the constant seeking and striving that had sometimes overwhelmed them.

My goal with this book is to take what I have learned from the hundreds of participants in these groups to guide you through this process, as best as human language can allow. You are at the precipice of falling in love with yourself, life, and spirit, and this guide serves as a map to your perhaps bewildering experiences. Hopefully, it helps you relax and feel safe, while providing context for what you experience.

By waking up to a greater realm of awareness—of what you're doing, feeling, and reacting to—you can start to shed your habitual egoic conditioning. You start relaxing into your more vulnerable, authentic self.

I believe that all of our challenges—personal and global—are based on the problem of separation from our spiritual nature. The solution is to move from this paradigm of our separate, struggling selves into the next phase of human development: a paradigm of non-separateness, where we live from a place of care and connection with the earth, society, and ourselves.

This is what embodied spiritual awakening offers us. It's not just that we solve these problems, but that we wake up to our spiritual connection to everyone and everything. From that paradigm of non-separation, what we choose to do is naturally in service to ourselves and others at the same time.

Reading the Signs of Awakening

Though embodied awakening is universal, it is experienced differently by every person. There are common signs of awakening, though, that you can look for in your everyday life. People start to feel more sensitive. They feel raw and exposed in life. Emotions such as grief, anger, and fear arise that can feel overwhelming at times. People start to ask deeper questions in life: "Who am I, why am I here, what's my purpose in life?"

A curiosity arises around the topic of awakening and

knowing who you are, which causes people to search for answers. They take a class or pick up a book like this. Many people entering the path of awakening begin to feel and recognize the pain of living as a separate self and the ache of loneliness—a disconnection from self, others, and the earth itself. A longing arises for deeper connections, authenticity, and meaning in life.

Sometimes the words I use to describe *Embodied Awakening* can sound esoteric and rarefied, simply because the experience itself is so profound. Just as it's hard to describe or understand falling in love until you actually experience it, explanations of spiritual transformation can seem merely intellectual if you have not experienced it yourself.

Having said that, whatever your mind thinks your spiritual awakening might be, your actual experience is likely to be different. It's sort of like when you're six and you're watching Cinderella—you think falling in love will be like that. As you grow up, you learn that your version of falling in love is completely different, even if the qualities are the same.

I hope the chapters in this book inform you about the general qualities of spiritual awakening, even if the particulars of *your* story are completely unique and miraculous to you. This general map of the journey can help you skillfully navigate your individual circumstances.

Debunking the Spirituality Myth

People often wonder, "What do I need to do to awaken? Do I need to meditate more? Do I need to give up my life and go join a monastery? How do I find this connection to spirit?"

The truth is that you don't need to do any one specific thing to awaken. You don't have to meditate for seven hours a day, or go on a retreat to Nepal. The key to awakening is relaxing into the circumstances of your everyday life. Yes, meditation can be helpful to recognize Fundamental Consciousness, but since it's always here, you can also recognize it in the background of every moment of your daily life. You can have a spiritual practice that is integrated into everyday life. When you do that, your daily life itself becomes a practice ground, in addition to whatever other practices you choose to do.

Awakening unfolds in the midst of everyday life by bringing greater awareness and unleashing your capacity to feel life more deeply. It unfolds through both your joys and sorrows: falling in love, taking in a magnificent view, having difficult conversations with your boss at work, interacting with your spouse at home, or experiencing the loss of a loved one. You start to feel into these experiences with your whole being.

As the Sufi mystic and poet Rumi said, "Don't go off to blue perfection." He was reminding people to not use spirituality as a way to escape life. Spirituality is not a drug that takes the pain of life away. It's a natural part of your wholeness that gives you space to host and feel the pain and joy of life in a fuller way. Rather than flattening life out, you gain more capacity to feel those ups and downs without running away, avoiding, or breaking down. You find more flow in the river of your life.

Reaching Within

My own experience of embodied awakening opened me to the infinite, but it didn't happen all at once.

My path started in early childhood. As an adopted child, I had an innate quest to know who I was. Something was missing, but I could not figure out what that could be. I had everything I could have wanted at the time—great parents, a beautiful home, a boyfriend I loved, and friends I cared about. I told myself, "You should be more grateful." Yet there was a gnawing emptiness and ennui that stalked me.

In my mid-twenties, I became driven by the quest for peace: peace within myself, peace with others, global peace, and peace with the environment. After being trained as a scientist in my undergrad work, I went to the University of Notre Dame to pursue a master's degree in international peace studies. In 1999, my partner, Kevin, and I opened a yoga studio to help other people find peace and well-being through yoga, meditation, and other spiritual practices.

When I was forty-three years old, Kevin and I separated. He was very analytical and rational, and I was discovering my spiritual side. It felt like we had grown apart. The challenge of owning a business also put pressure on our relationship, and we decided we needed to take a break. It was a very difficult time.

In the absence of my relationship with Kevin, all those foundational feelings I had once experienced—the ache of separation, the feeling that there was something wrong with me, the fear I wasn't enough—came rushing back. I was shocked. In the stillness of not being engaged in a relationship, the inner ache I had managed to silence reared its head again. I felt anxious, worried, and sad. I hadn't dealt with those emotions or processed them. I had bypassed them with a spiritual practice that never actually addressed those uncomfortable feelings.

In the aftermath of that realization, my regular distractions—the internet, good food, drinking, bicycling— stopped working to shift my state. Even yoga couldn't help me escape my discomfort.

But instead of questioning why, I thought that I wasn't trying hard enough. I did more yoga. I did stronger yoga. I thought if I just worked harder and pushed more, I would be able to lift myself up to find that bliss again. Instead, I felt more and more exhausted. At the time, I was an

Ashtanga yoga practitioner, so I added *Anusara* practice to my schedule, hoping that could help me overcome the knot of emotions within.

After a weekend Anusara yoga retreat, my teacher said, "Yoga is amazing. It just keeps getting better and better." I couldn't have agreed more. I felt so uplifted, and I left feeling totally at peace. But when I got home, I had a complete return to depression, and that feeling of peace slipped through my fingers like sand. The harder I tried to hold on, the faster it disappeared.

In that moment, I felt so much grief and shame. If my teacher was telling me life should just keep getting better and better, why was I feeling depressed? Was there something wrong with me?

After that workshop, I had a session with one of my awakening teachers. I don't remember the exact conversation, but the phone call went something like this:

In his soothing voice, he asked, "What would you like to work with today?"

"I just returned from a yoga workshop where I felt happy and joyful," I said. "Now I'm home and feeling sad and depressed. I just want to get back to the light."

"Go into the dark," he said. "Let the light find you."

He explained that being present and welcoming whatever was there was the pathway back to the light. I was running away instead of feeling what I was experiencing.

I had to embrace both the comfortable and uncomfortable feelings as part of my wholeness.

For the first time, I had permission and guidance on how to welcome the discomfort I was feeling. On my path of spiritual awakening, I learned that I was feeling the friction and tension of being both a finite human being and an infinite divine being. This ache signified that I was ready for my awakening journey.

As I gave myself permission to feel what I felt and engaged with different awakening teachers and embodied awakening paths, I started to do real inner work for the first time. I had the support of mentors and teachers, and also a therapist, who all helped me deal with my unprocessed past. I was primed and ready for real connection and engagement.

A few years later, I had my embodied awakening shift. As I walked across the floor at a workshop, I dropped into myself. I heard a *clunk* and felt my feet land on the earth, like I was wearing gravity boots on the moon. Immediately, I felt anchored into myself, anchored into the earth. I felt *here* and not separate from anyone or anything. There was a pervading sense of space, infinite being, and an abiding okayness for no reason.

For so many years I had used yoga to create a safe, transcendent, separate self. In that moment, all the sudden, the bubble burst and I found myself in the heart of life.

Everything felt close and intimate. I was glued into life in some new way, with no avenue for escape and a deep feeling of joy.

Surprisingly, it felt good. I felt alive. I could feel my body and infinite spirit as one.

A little while later, as part of that same workshop, we were asked to find a partner. I'm an introvert, and when they say, "Go find a partner," I always get anxious. But this time, when I felt the anxiety, there was so much space within me. I felt I was so much bigger than the room that was there, than my body, than the anxiety. Somehow, I felt completely okay *and anxious* at the same time. I had space to process and feel without being overwhelmed.

After the workshop, I went out and sat by a lake, just feeling all the changes I was experiencing. The sunlight was sparkling on the water, I felt a bubbling up of excitement inside myself, and as my excitement grew, the water began to sparkle more. There was a seamless confluence between my inner world and the outer world. The hawk overhead seemed to be flying inside of me—the bigger, more infinite me. I felt so connected to everything. The sacredness of life, including myself, was so apparent it brought tears of joy.

That spaciousness, connection, and peace continues to be the context for my life. At the previous level of peace I had known, I felt separate from life, even comforted by my distance from it. When I connected to the field through embodied awakening, that distance vanished. I felt more intimate, more authentic, more whole. I went from being a black-and-white stick figure of a person to a full-technicolor, 3D, whole person.

I was astounded by how much ease I felt as I integrated these new qualities into my daily life. I had the confidence to take greater risks and the capacity to handle greater joys and disappointments. With this new capacity, this Fundamental Consciousness, I could do the things I really wanted to do.

My spiritual awakening was intertwined with a deep process of healing and maturation. I reconciled with my former partner, Kevin, and I started guiding others through this journey of awakening.

I had also been searching for my biological parents for a long time, and I had a lead. I'd been avoiding calling that person because I was afraid to find out what they might know—or not know. After my awakening, I had a resilience and confidence that supported me in being able to handle bigger disappointments and bigger joys. I made that phone call I was previously terrified to make, a call that would eventually bring more joy and love into my everyday life.

Guiding Awakening

After I had my awakening, I was so excited about the transformation I had undergone that I wanted to share the path with everybody.

I began working with individuals and groups, guiding and encouraging them to share their life experiences and be held and seen as they traveled their spiritual path.

I continue to teach yoga as well as facilitating awakening groups, and have found my passion and purpose in sharing and creating supportive communities. The lessons we have learned in community are gathered here into the topics of this book.

- Obstacles to awakening: Discover the things that stand in your way, and how you can skillfully navigate your own awakening.

- Permission to be as you are: Allow yourself to be, and find your path to the real and authentic version of yourself.

- Embodiment: Get out of your head and into your body, to find an integration of the mental, physical, and spiritual.

- Fundamental Consciousness: Open up to the infinite nature of your own spirit, and find greater space and well-being to live life fully.

- Mutuality: Learn to honor your views and another person's views at the same time, letting the situation grow you both.

- Obstacles as path: Realize that comfortable and uncomfortable experiences are two sides of one coin of life, and that obstacles aren't a barrier, but a sacred part of the journey.

- Trauma: Heal your unprocessed past on the personal, intergenerational, and cultural levels.

- The core ache of separation: Understand that your feelings of depression and anxiety can be a normal sign that you are ready for spiritual awakening, not something to fear or feel shamed by.

- Awake living: Embrace the journey of awakening in the midst of daily life to bring more enjoyment and presence to every moment.

- Community: Understand the value of being in a community that will support your journey. A place where you are held in your wholeness—seen, heard, respected, and celebrated.

As a teacher, I've been blessed to witness the uniqueness of everyone's journey. I know that on the path of embodied awakening, no two people have exactly the same experience. No one else's awakening looked exactly like mine or exactly like any other's. Each has a unique flavor, but includes certain universal qualities that I describe in this book, which may help you understand your own journey no matter how it presents.

Throughout this book, I share many stories so that you

can see how awakening unfolds in different people's lives. Names have been changed, and sometimes identifying circumstances have been altered to preserve the privacy of my students. But the essence of the stories is all true, and I hope you will find inspiration and meaning in each one.

As you read this book, take time between each chapter to reflect on what it might mean in your life. Many chapters have practices—something concrete you can use to engage with the chapter topic. I recommend that you pause at the end of each chapter and see how that practice applies to your life.

As you take this journey and read through the chapters, consider moving in a sequential way. Our journey builds on itself, and each chapter lays a foundation that the next chapter adds to. However, if there's something you feel really drawn to, listen to and follow your inner impulses! Feel free to jump ahead to a chapter that calls to you.

By going slowly and digesting what's being presented, you give your body and mind time to integrate your learning. But sometimes when you've been parched, your soul is thirsty for awakening. If that's the case, it's okay to read quickly and take everything in before returning to the beginning to start the process of integration. Trust yourself and your impulses, and you can't do it wrong.

And as you walk this path, remember that this book is intended to supplement your awakening journey. It does not replace appropriate spiritual, medical, or professional support. Whether you read this guide alone or with the support of a loving community, your journey is yours alone to take. It can be terrifying at times, but I promise you, your newfound spirituality and wholeness will astound you.

As my students often say: "I wish I knew this three decades ago. I wish I had gone through this process so much earlier. It's such a better way to live!"

You will have more maturity, more choices, and more authenticity in all your relationships. You will find a whole new paradigm of living beyond the confines of the limited egoic self. Your journey begins now. And it all starts with understanding the obstacles to your awakening.

Chapter 2

OBSTACLES TO AWAKENING

Your task is not to seek for love, but merely to seek and find all the barriers within yourself that you have built against it.—Rumi

Finding Satisfaction

When Don was on his deathbed after having suffered a stroke, everything he had accomplished until then meant nothing. A man in his seventies, Don had achieved what most people in society would call a great life: a brilliant career, wonderful wife, children, big house, and all the material wealth that symbolized reaching the American Dream.

As Don lay in bed, wavering between life and death, he felt sad that he had not followed his longings to know who he was on a spiritual level. He lamented not listening to his inner voice through the decades, not making his spiritual connection a higher priority. But mostly, he felt deep regret that he might die without knowing who he truly was.

Miraculously, Don survived the stroke. When he left the hospital, he took the opportunity to follow the deep longing in his heart. He realized that the obstacle to knowing his spiritual self was grasping at pleasures in the material world, pursuing material pleasures as a substitute for the true satisfaction of spiritual awakening.

After his recovery, Don began to devote his time and energy to knowing himself at a deeper level. A few weeks later, he signed up for my awakening program. There, he learned that he was experiencing the first obstacle to awakening, which is not knowing our divine nature.

Spiritual awakening is about releasing the struggle that blocks your awakening. It's the process of rediscovering the essence of who you are in your divinity and embodying the full spectrum of your humanity. As you recognize who you truly are, the barriers to living a satisfied life naturally dissolve. You feel a greater sense of wholeness and completion. This brings you the ultimate satisfaction that is independent of life's situations.

Upgrading Your Spiritual Operating System

The awakening process creates a massive shift in the way you see the world. Imagine you have a computer running Windows 98. When you first bought it, you were pleased. It served its purpose and did everything you needed it to do. But now it's old and clunky and hasn't been updated in two decades. It can't run any of the newest programs or games. Its programming is obsolete.

That old computer isn't so different from most of us. The cool new programs of life are calling. Rather than struggling to make them work on our existing infrastructure, it's time to upgrade the operating system. When we Awaken, we appreciate the old program that protected our small, fragile, ego-based self, while recognizing that it no longer serves us.

The ego is our separate sense of self. It's the part of us that, in spiritual terms, struggles, strives, fears the unknown, and often perceives circumstances as a threat. We begin to develop our ego around the age of two. It is a necessary, natural, and important part of our whole self, and a crucial stage of human development. This sense of self is useful. Practical. It helps us separate from our parents and learn that we have our own needs and desires—that we are an independent self. It teaches us about who we are and what our place in the world is. As we grow, we take on ego-based conditioning designed to protect us.

But as we continue to mature, we reach a natural point where living from that small, separate sense of self is inadequate, inefficient, and painful. In the awakening process, as we realize we really are the more infinite, timeless essence of being, the ego can finally relax and we can serve something greater. We go through a spiritual awakening and, like a computer upgrading its operating system, we can run new programs that we simply could not run previously.

As we awaken, we're no longer trying to figure everything out with our minds alone. Instead, we open to a larger reality. There's less struggle and a greater sense of empowerment living from a larger field of our own being. We begin to live connected to all that is. Actions are no longer driven by a separate sense of self struggling to survive, but instead by an infinite sense of connection and fundamental well-being. From here, we act in ways that have more flow and less struggle.

Sometimes this transition into awakening is sudden—a dramatic shift that changes everything. More commonly, it is a slow, gradual recognition of changes taking place in how we perceive and respond to our lives.

It used to be quite common to see a crisis point reached around midlife, but these days it often happens much earlier. Some even use the term "quarter-life crisis" to explain why so many people begin searching for what is missing in their twenties or thirties. No matter what age it happens, most of us will eventually reach a point where we begin to question who we are, why we feel the way we do, and what is the deeper meaning of life.

But without guidance, it's easy to think that we are failing, falling apart, or losing our drive when we reach this sacred threshold of awakening. We fight to keep our old life and old way of struggle alive. We get scared and double down on our ego-driven life.

It's only natural. As human beings, we each carry an ego-based operating system that pushes us to avoid what's uncomfortable and soldier on. Our ego habitually moves us to gravitate toward what's easy. It keeps us spinning in fear and judgment, constantly hijacking us from joy and satisfaction.

Once we upgrade our operating system through awakening, though, we replace that conditioning with a new operating system that taps the entire universe. We find our connection to everyone and everything. We're operating from an infinite system, able to run greater programs of kindness and compassion. We're no longer operating on fear and survival, but instead on love and possibility.

When we awaken, we start to live from a place inside where we can feel our bodies and those of others around us. We are freer, able to move in a direction that serves us in the moment. We can live informed by the moment, embracing our creativity and following the direction that our life and our souls pull us toward.

Spiritual awakening is the next natural stage of human development.

Understanding the Obstacles in Your Path

Just because it's the next stage doesn't mean everything will be smooth. The Indian sage Patañjali knew this. Living around 300 BC, he is considered by many to be one of the fathers of yoga. He compiled the famous *Yoga Sutras*, a foundational sourcebook that codified important yogic concepts, especially in relation to the mind and spiritual awakening. According to the *Yoga Sutras,* there are five obstacles that lead to struggle in life.

These are called *kleshas*, a Sanskrit word that means "blocks or afflictions of the mind." Understanding the kleshas can help us see the territory of the awakening journey more clearly and give us compassion toward the self as we go through the natural challenges of the path. We learn to let go of the pain of living from an ego-based approach to life, which brings neurosis, struggle, exhaustion, and existential angst. Ultimately, we wake up to find greater freedom.

The five kleshas are:

1. *Avidya*—not knowing our divine nature.

2. *Asmita*—the ego, which creates a separate sense of self.

3. *Raga*—grasping and chasing pleasure.

4. *Dvesha*—avoidance of pain.

5. *Abhinivesha*—fear of death and change.

I'm going to come back to avidya, and you'll see why in a moment. We'll begin with asmita. Asmita is the "I" maker, the ego. It's our sense of a separate self that makes us believe we are isolated from the outside world. Asmita makes us feel small. It tricks us into believing we are separate from everyone and everything.

Next comes raga. Raga means to grasp. This is the instinct I described earlier that drives the mind to grasp after what's pleasurable. It is the root of addiction, and a byproduct of living from an ego-based separate sense of self.

Fourth is dvesha. It's aversion—a repulsion toward and pushing away of what's unpleasant. It is the other side of raga. We grasp with one hand and push with the other. Dvesha is the source of our procrastination. It also underlies the hatred that exists in our world.

Abhinivesha is the fifth klesha. It is often translated as a fear of death, and it's a fear of deep or meaningful change. Change is at the heart of the human condition and a necessary part of spiritual awakening, but abhinivesha pushes us away from that and toward struggling to keep our lives and ourselves from changing.

Together, these kleshas describe the challenge of mind-based egoic living and the tendencies that arise in living from a separate sense of self. In the early part of life, we grow accustomed to living in accordance with these tendencies. But eventually, we hit a point where we recognize we're struggling. We try to get away from anxiety and worry, but we can't.

We struggle to grasp satisfaction by clicking on the next computer ad, but deep satisfaction eludes us. The old ways are no longer working in our life, but we are afraid to step out and try something new. We live in a well of dissatisfaction, and we start to wonder if there is something more. We ask, "How can I find more ease and grace and enjoyment in life?"

But what about the first klesha? Avidya is the sense that we don't know who we really are as human beings. We've lived from the mind as if that's who we are, and it keeps us spinning in cycles of frustration, existential angst, and emptiness. The first klesha tells us that the reason we're living with such struggle is that we're unaware of the truth of our divine selves, our infinite nature.

Walking the Path to Connection

The five kleshas each explain a certain stage of life that precedes awakening. Mind-based ego conditioning serves us well during the first part of life, but becomes limiting, painful, and frustrating once we are in the second part of life. At its heart is *samsara,* the Sanskrit notion of living from a sense of separate self. Samsara is mind-based living.

The Cycle of Samsara

Samsara creates a cycle of suffering as we constantly find out that, in fact, pain is not avoidable. Every time we are struck with pain we feel it completely anew, along with a sense of betrayal or disappointment that our pleasure has once again been disrupted.

We can wake up to a larger sense of self, our true self, through the path of embodied awakening. When we do this, we are no longer dominated by the ego, or by samsara. The ego starts to relax, and we begin to see ourselves as part of a larger whole. Our identity shifts from the mind to the larger essence of our being.

The goal here is not to kill the ego. It's to wake up to the point where we know ourselves as Fundamental Consciousness, the essence of who we are. When we do that, our ego relaxes into serving something greater. It's important to realize that the ego is not inherently bad. It's not wrong. It's just a very limited part of self.

In the first part of our lives, we want to build a strong ego, it's essential for being a healthy human being. But in the second part of life, it's not meant to run the whole show of our life, and when we let it, that's when we begin to struggle. We're using this tiny part of ourselves to run a life that's meant to be run from a much larger operating system.

As the ego-based mind begins to serve our greater self, we open ourselves up to an entirely new way of living life.

We no longer live from the prison of the mind-based ego and instead relax into a larger field of Being and an awakening life, finding enlightenment.

But how do we learn to walk that path?

Conditioning and Spiritual Awakening

Often at the start of a spiritual path, we approach it with a conventional mindset of trying to be a good person (as opposed to a bad person). We think we have to learn how to be a good person. We think, "I should be generous, I should be kind, I should be open." We use spiritual conditioning to improve ourselves and try to reach that noble goal.

But spiritual awakening is not a path of self-improvement; it is a path of spiritual realization, where you realize your whole self, the parts you like *and* the parts you dislike.

It's like riding a tricycle as a small child. It's the best thing ever at that age, the ultimate joy. Then you naturally upgrade to a bicycle, and maybe later to a car. Your desire for satisfaction keeps moving forward.

The same is true of your spiritual journey.

When you awaken, you naturally grow into another operating system. You wake up to the totality of who you are. You come to understand and embrace that sometimes you might feel generous, but sometimes you might feel selfish. Sometimes you might feel kind, but sometimes you might feel defensive. You learn to embrace the totality of your humanity and relax into who and what you are. You wake up to the essence of your being.

What Is Spiritual Bypassing?

Spiritual bypassing is a term that was coined by psychologist John Welwood, who defined it as our tendency to use spiritual ideas and practices to sidestep or avoid facing unresolved emotional issues, psychological wounds, and unfinished developmental tasks.

When you engage in spiritual bypassing, you avoid dealing with what's uncomfortable in your life and escape into Fundamental Consciousness. It's easy to fall into this because the behavior isn't problematic in itself. It's only a problem when you allow it to take over and distract you from facing uncomfortable truths.

Don, the stroke survivor who left the hospital determined to listen to his inner spiritual longings, relaxed into who he was. Through his work in my awakening program, he learned to feel more deeply and welcome his feelings. He stopped fighting with life and settled into his body, where he woke up to the essence of who and what he was. It brought the greatest joy to his heart to settle into the deep, infinite, timeless place within himself.

Awakening to this spiritual nature of your being and all of life allows more space to welcome a greater awareness of your human frailty and shortcomings. It allows you more space to see, feel, and include the more troubling, under-developed parts of yourself. This inclusivity lets you work creatively and intelligently with the challenges that you face. There's a sense of not just waking up to who you are, to your divinity, but also growing up, growing into the higher stages of adult development. You become a more capable and competent human being.

Releasing the Struggle

One of the things you become more capable of handling on the path of awakening is difficult emotions. People often discover that avoiding the uncomfortable parts of self, and fighting against the way life is, starts to feel more painful than finally facing and feeling the pain they've been running from. The treadmill of reaching for satisfaction from outside becomes exhausting, and you begin to crave a calmer, inner joy.

Spiritual awakening allows you to relax the ego and open into a larger sense of self. There you find more nourishment and more support. There is a deep, profound, and calming knowing—and, of course, less struggle! You are at peace. When you stop fighting life and grasping after life, you can relax into facing, feeling, and enjoying life.

An obstacle in the old operating system is not giving yourself permission to be who you fully are. Yes, challenges and discomforts will arise, but once you wake up to know who you are, you have more space and capacity to welcome yourself and your life as it is. You're living from the fullness of your being. Allowing yourself to be as you are is the next step in the journey of embodied awakening.

Chapter 3

PERMISSION TO BE AS YOU ARE

Allow yourself to feel whatever you are feeling.—Jon Kabat-Zinn

The Sea Monster

If you find yourself fighting your own emotions, trying to be happy when you feel sad or peaceful when you're afraid, it could be that you haven't fully given yourself permission to be as you are.

In the early days of my yogic education, one of my teachers told me the myth of Krishna and Kaliya. Kaliya was a sea monster who lived in the river Yamuna. The townspeople in the surrounding town of Vrindavan relied on the river for their livelihood. It gave them water to drink, to cook their food, and to bathe in.

But sometimes, people would go down to the river . . . and were never seen again.

The villagers began to fear that a deadly sea monster

was living in the river, eating the villagers. They started to avoid the river, which had once given them such bounty. They were terrified, but they dared not tell one of the most revered persons who lived in the town. The young boy, Krishna, was considered an incarnation of the Divine. The villagers feared that if the brave boy learned about the sea monster, he would go to the river to battle it. They didn't want Krishna himself to be killed. In their desire to protect him, the villagers withheld the truth from their revered god-boy.

As people avoided the river, dirty dishes piled up. Clothes went unwashed. Despite their secrets, Krishna eventually discovered the truth behind Why the villagers were avoiding the Yamuna River. As soon as he heard the rumors about a sea monster, Krishna ran down to the river and dove into the water to fight the sea monster. The villagers followed him and gathered by the shore to help protect Krishna. But all they could do was watch from the shore.

Krishna and the sea monster fought so hard they churned up the river. Up they went, and down again. Then with a great heave the monster wrapped around Krishna and dove down, down, into the water. There was a moment of total silence. Every villager held their breath as the water grew still. A few bubbles rose to the surface and popped. Then nothing.

The villagers began to weep. It seemed like their worst fears had come true.

As the villagers turned away from the water, heading home, they were shocked by a magnificent sight. Krishna emerged from the water on the back of the sea monster, playing his flute. Exhausted, the great serpent collapsed onto the sand and closed its eyes.

The townspeople grabbed their sickles and shovels, ready to rush in and kill the monster. With blade and tool they would behead it!

But Krishna held them back with a look. He climbed down from the monster's back and walked calmly up to her face. She could have swallowed him in a single bite, but Krishna was not afraid. He put away his flute and told the monster, "Our little river is too small for you to live in. What if I take you out to the big sea, where you will have all the space you need to be you?"

Kaliya smiled and nodded. So Krishna climbed once more on her back, and showed her the way to the sea. The villagers rejoiced, because Krishna had saved them. They saw the kindness that Krishna gave to Kaliya, how he honored her and helped her to get what she needed.

One way to interpret the story is that Kaliya represents our "monstrous" emotions. So often we don't know how to feel our feelings, and that makes them seem terrifying. We want to kill them, to defeat them, to overcome them. In so doing, we often create havoc for the people around us—biting their heads off with our own unprocessed anger.

When you give your difficult emotions room to flow and be in the ocean of Fundamental Consciousness—the infinite, timeless essence of your own being—they become a beautiful, sacred part of your wholeness. Permission to feel what you feel and be as you are is the pathway into awakening. The old paradigm was to kill your monstrous emotions, but that only set you at war with yourself. You can learn to allow all of your feelings, even the ones that sometimes feel monstrous.

Learning to Be Yourself

Permission to be as you are is a powerful gateway into spiritual awakening. When you embrace who you are, you gracefully grow from the ground of who you are into the field of who you are becoming. It's natural.

You have the strength to release the habit of going to war with yourself. Instead of pushing yourself to be different than who you are, allow yourself to feel—to be as you are—and let yourself grow from there. Permission gives you space to embrace the wholeness of yourself. To be happy and sad, to be angry and calm, to be scared and courageous.

If you're constantly at war with yourself, you waste your energy and attention on trying to be different. That's why you're exhausted. Instead, the invitation is to take time to befriend yourself, to sit down to metaphysical tea with yourself and your emotions. Allow yourself to be as you are. Bring compassion, care, and love to yourself exactly as you are right now. When you do that, your whole nervous system can relax and open to recognize the essence of who you are. You savor your tea.

The Flavors of Life

A big part of the process of giving yourself permission is embracing your feelings. In the yogic tradition, your feelings are called *rasas*, which translates roughly to "the flavors of life." The journey of spiritual awakening, from this embodied yogic perspective, is a journey to taste all the flavors of life.

Yogic tradition identifies nine basic emotions, which are depicted in a wheel. The nine emotions are love, joy, wonder, peace, anger, courage, sadness, fear, and disgust. These emotions each represent a flavor of life, like oregano, salt, or basil. Many of us try to cut off unpleasant emotions, but just like a full palette of flavors gives us a rich experience of food, the full palette of emotions is important to give us a rich experience of living.

When we fight our emotions, such as trying not to be sad when we're grieving, or denying fear when we're afraid, we use up valuable energy. The uncomfortable feelings do not go away—they simply lodge in our bodies, creating more tension.

Part of the journey of life is becoming aware of the unconscious habit of avoiding uncomfortable feelings. This habit creates war within yourself. If you are feeling sad, and you try to pretend that you're happy, you create conflict within your system. The suppressed emotions get buried deep in your body tissues and wait for another time to come up to be fully felt and released. As they say, your issues are stored in your tissues.

To diffuse that inner struggle, the invitation is to befriend yourself. Meet yourself where you are, and accept your emotions no matter which "monstrous" feelings you are experiencing. Give yourself permission to feel—to taste all of the flavors of life.

Allowing Yourself to Be

This concept of giving yourself permission to feel is the key to embodied spiritual awakening. When you block your feelings, you do so in a very physical way. You tense your entire body, trying to capture the feeling and hold it there. Think about being a little kid and feeling embarrassed. You don't want to start crying, so you clench your whole body.

That's what we do as adults, and it's a problem because our body is the instrument through which we wake up to Fundamental Consciousness. If our instrument is tight and shut down because we're trying not to feel, we're not going to be able to attune to the essence of who we are.

Yoga is a great way to connect with your body and open up. But if you're holding emotions down with every fiber of your being, yogic stretching won't be enough to release that tension. You have to allow your nervous system to relax, allow your feelings, which are just energy, to move freely through your body again. That means being in a practice where you're giving yourself time and space to feel your feelings, moment to moment.

When I run my awakening workshops, I always ask my students, "How many people here were given permission, in your family of origin, to feel all your feelings?" Usually, not a single person raises their hand. Most people, especially in older generations, weren't given permission to be sad or to be afraid. They were told, "Good girls don't get angry," or "Good boys don't get sad." When they were afraid, they were told, "Be a big boy, be a big girl, get over it."

If we tell our friends, "I'm scared," they usually just try to boost us up. "Oh, you're so great. You have no reason to be afraid. You're just such an amazing person." They think they're being kind, being helpful, but they're really reiterating that inner attitude that fear is bad, and we are weak when we feel it. It's no wonder we start to tell ourselves these same things. We think "getting over it" is courage and fear is weakness.

We don't know how to be with and feel uncomfortable feelings, so we try to bypass them. The problem is . . . we can't actually do that. We may think we're avoiding feelings, but really, we're just cramming them further down, leaving unprocessed, undigested emotions in our system. They don't go away. They just become harder to access, and they gum up our entire system and cause the mind to go into hyper-speed—even creating a type of existential anxiety, where we are afraid but not sure what we're afraid of anymore.

Practicing Feeling

What do you do when it's difficult to feel your feelings, but you don't want to push them away? There are a few different techniques you can practice.

When you feel challenged by a difficult feeling, just stop. Take a deep breath and place your hand directly over your heart. Tell yourself, either out loud or in your head, "Wow. It's really difficult to feel this right now. But I give myself permission to feel it." You can get really specific, naming the emotion you're feeling and even why it's hard to feel. "This pain hurts so much, but I allow myself to feel it because it's part of my wholeness," or "It's really difficult to feel angry, but I give myself permission." Sometimes just feeling the warmth of your own human hand on your heart can bring a little bit of comfort.

Another great feeling practice is to give yourself compassion and love. Kristin Neff has a beautiful three-step self-compassion practice that I use with my students, and they find it really empowering. You can follow this any time you're struggling not to be at war with yourself.

1. Recognize that this is a difficult moment. You're suffering. You're having a hard time.

2. Remind yourself that others feel this way too. You are not alone. Often we think, "Oh my god, I'm the only person feeling anxious—everybody else has it together." The truth is other people feel the way you do. They're also hiding it, fighting that inner war.

3. Finally, give yourself words of comfort. Again, you can say these out loud or you can just think them, whichever makes you more comfortable. Say, "I'm here," or "It's okay." Pair this with a gesture of comfort, which could be the hand on the heart, or hugging yourself, or even a fist bump! Do whatever feels natural to you.

As you get onto the path of spiritual awakening, you may notice that allowing yourself to feel can bring up extreme emotions. This is especially true if you're uncovering childhood trauma or acknowledging long-repressed emotions, or even connecting to a shared cultural trauma.

We'll discuss wounds more when we talk about trauma, but for now, it's enough to know that this opening up to feelings is a natural part of the path to awakening. A lot of people say, "Oh my god, why is this stuff coming up?" They see the emotions as a problem to solve, rather than an experience to move through.

You are a sensitive person already—that's why you're still reading this book—and sometimes suppressing feelings is one thing people do to try not to be sensitive and feel. This process of feeling your feelings doesn't make you overly sensitive; it allows you to feel the original feelings you pushed down

When that happens, don't be afraid to lean on other people. We are designed to feel our feelings with other attuned humans. Being with another person with a well-regulated nervous system actually helps us regulate our own nervous system. Having professional help can be impactful. If you don't want to go that route, try to find a friend or family member who can listen and be there. Just make sure they aren't trying to fix the problem. You *want* to feel these feelings!

There's nothing wrong, even if you're feeling sad or angry or any other range of uncomfortable emotions. It's all a normal part of being human. It's part of being mature and grown-up to experience the full spectrum of human emotions.

Like the story of the sea monster Kaliya, you're learning to accept who you are and finding ways to be yourself in peace.

> **Words to Live By**
>
> This, too, is a sacred part of my wholeness.

Feeling It All

As you begin this journey of opening up, remember that in your awakening process you can open to feel more than one feeling at once. Living from the ego-based mind, you can usually only be aware of one emotion at a time (if any at all). But after awakening, you have the space to hold many emotions at the same time, giving a fullness to your experiences and allowing you not to be overwhelmed by any single emotion. You are big enough to host them all.

When people work with me, they sometimes come in saying, "I'm so angry!" They're consumed by that one emotion. As we work together, they have the capacity to embrace other emotions. They are not just angry, but also sad. Not just apathetic, but also caring.

As you open to your essence you have more space to host multiple feelings at once—even opposite feelings, which I call the paradox. To be both happy and sad at the same time about different things in your life (or even the very same thing!), expands your field of awareness. When you can do that, it means that you've opened to have more access to your true nature, to the spaciousness of your being.

It's also okay, and can be very helpful at times, to choose to distract yourself from feeling any emotion. You can choose to set a feeling aside and come back to it later. For example, if you're in a meeting at work and something makes you feel sad, you can acknowledge it, set it aside so you can finish your presentation or your work, and then come back to that feeling later, when you have the time to give it the attention it deserves.

Ultimately, the more you learn to feel, the more space and capacity you have to feel. In the beginning it may be hard to give yourself permission to feel what you feel, but like Kaliya moving into the sea, the more you practice feeling your feelings, the more space they have to breathe and move. When you awaken to realize your true essence as Fundamental Consciousness, you have a larger sea of being in which to feel your feelings. It gets easier. You feel more flow. It starts to feel natural. And most people report that it's such a better, more relaxed, and empowering way to live.

Finally, it's important to note that feeling an emotion is not the same thing as acting it out. Giving yourself permission to feel angry and allowing that energy to flow through your body is not the same as giving yourself permission to pick up a baseball bat and break someone's windshield. Feel your feelings, but feel them within. Otherwise, you'll end up like Kaliya, drowning villagers just because they're unlucky enough to be close to her thrashing.

In the next chapter, we'll learn to experience our feelings more fully by moving into our bodies. We'll physically notice our feelings, instead of staying only in our minds, and discover the joy and peace of embodiment.

Chapter 4

EMBODIMENT

If you were in your body, you'd be home by now.
—bumper sticker seen by Tosha Silver

Hiding Stress in the Body

How connected are you to your body? When you feel or think something, are you aware of how that feels in your body?

Jenny was a woman in her late forties who worked in executive leadership at a large corporation in the defense industry. She was one of the only women in a position of power and authority in her industry, a titan at the office. It was a very high-achieving, demanding job, and she was very good at it. But despite all of her career success, she felt untethered. She was lost in her job and yearning for something more.

Jenny came to work with me because of this longing for something more and a generalized anxiety she couldn't pin down. At our awakening sessions, I would invite her to close her eyes and feel into her body.

When she thought about being anxious, I asked, "What sensations do you feel in your body?"

Jenny noticed that she felt a tension in her belly, a tightness. We sat together and I coached her to feel this tension, this tightness, and not to try to make it go away, not to try to make it be different. I invited her to come into relationship with the sensation.

As she sat with these various emotions and pockets of tension, her awareness moved from thoughts in her mind to sensations in her body. Like an ice cube in a warm bath, those areas of tension slowly melted back into the totality of her being. And when that happened, she settled more deeply into herself and felt more relaxed. Not because she got rid of the anxiety, but because she came into relationship with the tension, felt it, and honored it. As it melted, it became part of her wholeness.

By the end of our first session, Jenny said to me, "I feel more here. I feel more settled in the couch. Like I've really landed here in my body and in myself." Her mind, which she called her mariachi band, was full of little thoughts that were constantly going off and playing their music. But when she settled into herself and opened up to feel the tension and relaxation in her body, her wild thoughts melted away. The mariachi band stopped playing, and her mind was calm.

Instead of running the same old sixty thousand thoughts each day, her mind was then open and available for new creative thoughts. She could initiate new movements in life.

After about a year of working with me, Jenny realized that the career success and monetary reward of her job was no longer fulfilling. Her job was making her tense, stressed and unfulfilled, and she had desires that she wasn't honoring. She decided it was time to leave. Instead, she wanted to follow her calling and pursue something more meaningful to her.

Jenny started to ask the deeper questions in life: "Who am I? How can I serve more? How can I better use my gifts and talents to serve?" She realized, "Awakening has allowed me to see new possibilities."

Jenny unfolded the essence of who she was, and decided to open her own private coaching practice. There she uses the same skills in a satisfying way, one that's more in line with her drives and passion. She has more energy, feels more relaxed, and has let go of those pockets of hidden tension.

An embodied awakening is about recognizing our wholeness. It means being aware of our feelings in our bodies again—not just our emotions, but also our physical sensations. Like Jenny, as we land in our physical bodies more, we become instruments for our awakening journey. The body becomes a vehicle for realizing Fundamental Consciousness—the essence of who we are.

Getting Physical

When you awaken, you become more intimate with not only what you're thinking, but also what you're feeling. That means the emotions we discussed earlier, and it also means the physical sensations of the body.

But something blocks us from connecting with our physical selves: the habit of living in our heads. Our identity merges with the thinking mind, at the expense of connection to other aspects of ourselves. Living from an ego-based mind creates a sense of separation. Part of awakening is the slow journey to drop down out of the exclusive identification with the thinking mind, and start to feel the breath and the body—opening to receive the sensations of tension and ease, heaviness and lightness, the signals of the body.

In the past, your mind may have been a great refuge from feeling the pain of life. Thank goodness we have that survival mechanism. It's a life-saving ability. But at some point in your journey, it can become detrimental. You start to feel lonely. You feel anxious and worried, and you feel a deep sense of dissatisfaction that the mind is constantly trying to resolve.

The result of disembodiment is an overstimulation of the mind. If you feel like you can't turn your mind off, that you're constantly worrying, it's probably because you're trapped in the room of the mind. You're not moving between the rooms in the mansion of your being.

When you're ready for awakening, you start to drop into your body. You feel your own feet on the floor, your hips in the chair, the movement of your breath, and the moment-to-moment experience of life. The mind can relax and be open to new information. It's not meant to be constantly working. Instead, you are designed to be present in a whole-being way.

Embodiment is the experience of coming home to yourself, of landing again in your body. It is a slow, gradual process of befriending your internal world. It's about dropping through the mental body and into the physical, and learning to inhabit yourself fully.

YOUR OTHER BODIES

In yogic traditions, we have many bodies. We have a mental body, a physical body, an emotional body, an energy body, and a spiritual body. Each of these bodies exists within us like layers of nested Russian dolls. The spiritual body is the part of us that feels open, free, and interconnected to everyone and everything.

Living exclusively in the mental body, or mind, leaves you feeling partial, like something is missing—because it is. When you learn to include all of your bodies in the totality of your being, you feel whole and complete. You tap into a sense of beingness when there's a coherence in your systems. This harmony arises from inhabiting all of your bodies at once, and it's a product of spiritual awakening.

In the process of spiritual awakening, you become more interested in and curious about what's going on inside your inner world. You're able to feel emotions and sensations inside your body. You function better, relate to other people better, and find a greater sense of belonging in life. You're more at ease and more capable.

Relaxing the Mind

One of the main benefits of embodied awakening is that the mind can relax into its rightful role to support the other aspects of your wholeness. The mind can stop trying to be the master of the house.

Picture your being like a mansion. We all need to sleep, and that means spending a lot of time in your bedroom. But if you spent *all* of your time in your bedroom, you would quickly start to have problems. You wouldn't be able to get food from the kitchen. You wouldn't be able to bathe yourself or take care of basic needs in the bathroom. You might not even be able to see friends and family, who likely spend their time in the living room or family room.

Your being is the same way. Like the restful bedroom, your mind is an important part of you, but it isn't the only part. You are invited to connect with your emotions and your energy, as well as your body. You can relax the mind from overworking—get out of the bedroom and use the rest of the house.

Embodiment doesn't mean that your mind stops working anymore than leaving your bedroom means you'll never sleep again. The opposite is actually true. Your mind works more optimally because it's connected to the whole of your being. If you're living in your head, you're constantly guessing at the whole picture, relying on an incomplete picture pieced together from the limited information you have.

> Your mind works more optimally because it's connected to the whole of your being.

If you were in your kitchen and someone asked you what color the floor was, you would just look down. But if you were across the street, having lemonade on your neighbor's porch, and they asked you the same question? You have to remember—or guess.

The same is true when you live in your head. You guess at what's going on with another person instead of feeling in your body and the body of the other person to know what's going on. Living in the mind disconnects us from a deeper, more primordial level of knowing. It leaves the mind trying to figure out things it can't know. This creates never-ending cycles of anxiety, rumination, and exhaustion.

Embodiment brings you into the mansion of your body of sixty trillion cells. When you drop into your body, you can notice your physical sensations, mental thoughts, and emotions. You have a bigger operating system that notices all these in your physical body. Instead of constantly trying to guess what you need, you can be in your body, listening to it, having a conversation with it. When you do that, you know precisely what you need, whether that is food, rest, or movement.

Listening to the Body's Intelligence

There's a deep wisdom and intelligence to the body, but most of us have become disconnected from it. We've been overtrained to use the thinking mind, and we've been discouraged from inhabiting our body and feeling our feelings.

The fact is that embodiment doesn't come naturally. It's something we all have to train for by giving ourselves permission to pause in life and notice what we're feeling in our bodies.

Some people might think that athletes are embodied, but

many athletes I've worked with treat the body as a machine. They push their bodies to do incredible feats, at the expense of listening to the body itself. Their mental goals for success often override the wisdom of their own bodies.

Often people say, "Oh, but I'm embodied. I do yoga." But *using* your body isn't the same as *being in* your body. As one of my clients so wisely said to me, "I used to use my body like a power tool" to get things done in life. A power tool doesn't have feelings and needs, but our human body does.

I had a yoga practice for at least ten years before I started to understand and embrace embodiment and began to feel and honor my body. When I started my journey to awakening, I actually had to decrease how much yoga I was doing. I realized I had been telling my body to perform, instead of listening to it speak. I was using my yoga practice, as well as running and other exercise, as a way to bypass uncomfortable feelings. My goal was to get out of my body, to escape the discomfort I felt. It was the best I knew at the time, and it helped me in my journey at that point. But it was also exhausting and unsustainable. My awakening journey enabled me to be with my uncomfortable feelings.

The awakening journey is a path of inclusion, coming into relationship with what has previously been pushed away; it's a journey of coming back into the body to listen to and honor its intelligence.

Noticing Sensations

One way of listening to your body is noticing sensations in your physical being by getting curious. Curiosity is a powerful catalyst to meeting yourself. When you invite curiosity, you explore.

The idea of sensations as the felt sense of your body was coined by Eugene Gendlin in his book *Focusing*. As he described it, there's a felt sense in your body in response to everything you do. Reading or listening to this book right now, there's a sensation happening in your body. That might be a tightness or a relaxation, it might be a heaviness or a lightness, it might be a buzzing, or it might be heat. Whatever it is, it's physically felt through your senses when you actually pay attention.

Here are ten possible sensations to be aware of as you learn to connect with your physical body:

1. Heaviness
2. Lightness
3. Tension
4. Openness
5. Buzzing energy, movement, flow
6. Numbness, vacancy, emptiness
7. Cold
8. Warmth
9. Imploding
10. Expanding

One easy way to feel your sensations is to clap your hands twenty times, very quickly and very hard. Then close your eyes and feel your fingers. Perhaps you feel a buzzing or energy in your fingertips, or a numbness?

Even though the motion is over, the body remembers, and it communicates that to you. The body is constantly communicating to us through sensation, but we haven't learned to listen. A big piece of embodiment is becoming intimate with our sensations.

WHERE DO YOU KEEP YOUR TENSION?

The body has many places where it holds anxiety, stress, and emotions, including these areas:

- Head
- Neck
- Shoulders
- Heart
- Belly
- Hips

Though these are the most common places to store your tension, you can store unfelt feelings anywhere in the body.

Leading from the Physical to the Spiritual

In *hatha* yoga, we always start with the physical body. "Spread your toes, step your feet apart." Everybody can do that. Then we start to work with our other bodies, each of which is more subtle and refined. Physical embodiment becomes the portal that leads to the other layers of being. It is the instrument through which we recognize Fundamental Consciousness. When that awakening happens, we can remain connected to the infinite, timeless aspect of self even while walking through life, because all aspects of our selves are perfectly integrated.

As we become more intimate with our bodies, they become home. The body becomes the center from where we meet life, right behind our eyes. Sometimes we meet life from beside ourselves. We even have that phrase, "Oh, that person—she's beside herself." But when we become intimately connected to our emotions and the felt sense that those emotions have in our body, we find alignment.

Think of it as meeting yourself. You're learning to be intimate with what you're feeling. You're checking into your emotions, and then continuing on and asking what you sense in your body. You can ask yourself these questions:

- Where do you feel tight?
- Where do you feel open?
- Where do you feel heavy?
- Where do you feel light?

Give yourself permission not to change it or try to make it different. This isn't about fixing it. Learn to just feel, to be intimate with yourself as you are. The more you become used to it, like any practice, the easier it will become.

FALLING INTO YOUR BODY

When my students take on this practice, they start to drop into their physical bodies. Sometimes, they even fear the experience. But this is part of the process of embodied awakening.

If you experience this fear, a great way to work with it is to start small. Go inside, feel your breath, feel a little bit of the sensations in your body, and then go back out into life and let yourself rest.

Don't make this an aggressive task—awakening requires self-kindness and self-respect. Start by respecting and honoring where you are right now, and then continue with little increments of greater connection and intimacy with yourself.

The more you meet yourself, your inner sensations, and your emotions, the more gently you'll fall into your body, the more deeply you'll land in yourself, and the more fully you'll open into a ground of security.

As you learn to listen to your body and cultivate this deeper intimacy with yourself, it will begin to affect everything you do. Sometimes it can feel like you're up in the bleachers looking at people on the playing field. But when you drop into your body, you're right in the center of the field, on the starting line. You're *here*, and that changes everything. It brings an immediacy to life, a fulfillment and an enjoyment that you don't have when you're separate from life. Intimacy with your body becomes intimacy with life.

Awakened Practice

One practice to invite curiosity is to sit with yourself at four different levels:

1. Physical sensations: Is the body or breath heavy, light, etc.?

2. Emotions: Are you sad, angry, happy, afraid, etc.?

3. Mind: Is it busy, open, ruminating, etc.?

4. Spaciousness of being: Can you relax and open to notice the witnessing part of yourself, the spacious awareness that's noticing all these other parts?

As you learn to witness and notice these parts of yourself, you start to have a little more space to allow things to be as they are. That gives sensations, emotions, and thoughts space to move and change inside of you. You are no longer hijacked by them. And you begin to experience a greater spaciousness of being where you feel infinite, peaceful, and okay for no reason!

By listening to all parts of yourself, you begin to access the least visible, but the most infinite of the Russian dolls—Fundamental Consciousness—who you really are. The next chapter will focus on opening to this Fundamental Consciousness that is the essence of your being.

Chapter 5

FUNDAMENTAL CONSCIOUSNESS

Because fundamental consciousness pervades our whole body, it's our deepest contact with our own individual self.—Judith Blackstone, PhD

Embracing a Heart Awakening

The field of Fundamental Consciousness interconnects us all. It's always here, but it isn't always easy to tap into.

Justin was a hyperrational man with a sharp intellect. However, like many of us living in modern society, and despite his loving family, he felt closed off, depressed, and isolated in his life. When Justin joined my awakening group, I assigned a practice called gazing. Basically, I asked him to look at himself in the mirror and just be.

Justin explored this gazing practice unexpectedly, while holding his six-month-old granddaughter in his arms. He stood before the mirror, looking at himself and noticing his reflection looking back at him. He felt entranced in that experience. Suddenly, he noticed in the mirror that his granddaughter was also looking at his reflection. She was participating in the gazing practice.

Justin was surprised and delighted. He then looked directly down at her, and she looked directly up at him. In that moment, his heart exploded into a field of love. He felt an incredible connection to her, and it opened him not only to a love for her in a completely new and different way, but to all of life.

This experience was a heart awakening. It wasn't that Justin suddenly loved his granddaughter more. It was a quantum shift that expanded his heart into a love for all creation. He found connection and contentment. When his heart opened, Justin experienced the field of Fundamental Consciousness. In this process, he became more vulnerable, connected, loving, present, and available. He discovered that his life was juicier, richer, and more fulfilling.

You cannot make yourself awaken to recognize Fundamental Consciousness—the essence of who and what you are that connects you to everyone and everything. It happens naturally, in its own time. But practices such as gazing and meditation can help you relax into that spontaneous awakening. It's your birthright to wake up and know who you are as a divine human being, and that comes through the realization of Fundamental Consciousness.

Awakening into the Infinite Lake

The Buddhist tradition shares this analogy to explain the journey of awakening to your yourself as Fundamental Consciousness: if you have a teaspoon of salt, put it in a shot glass of water, and drink it, it will be too bitter. You'll immediately have to spit it out. If, on the other hand, you stand in front of a freshwater lake, put a teaspoon of salt in it, and drink directly from the lake, the salt is so diluted that you can barely taste it, if at all.

Your emotions are like the salt in the water. Once you access Fundamental Consciousness, you experience your emotions from a more infinite perspective. You can still feel the sadness or anxiety, but it's less intense. Like the salt in the lake, you can still taste it, but it's less overwhelming.

As Fundamental Consciousness becomes your identity, the mind and the ego can relax. You're able to be more present to yourself, as well as to other people. You respond in new creative ways rather than just recreating the habits of the past. You become spacious, infinite, timeless, and aware.

This awakening is a must-have, an essential nutrient that we don't know we're missing. It brings with it resilience to life's hardships and struggles, and the capacity to feel life fully and participate fully from a well-resourced Infinite part of ourselves.

Most of us live our lives unaware of this aspect of ourselves. Life feels painful, difficult. It becomes too intense. Even enjoyable emotions often feel overwhelming. We feel limited, anxious, afraid. It's hard to be with our emotions because there's not enough space. They feel bigger than us.

Waking up is the process of realizing this sacred part of yourself and beginning to live *from* it as your identity. Fundamental Consciousness is the fabric of existence. It's already interpenetrating every cell of your being and every aspect of life, and it's always been there. It operates in the background, registering the world and your place in it. It observes your breath, the words you're speaking, the thoughts you're having. It is aware, all the time, of every given moment.

Opening Your Three Centers

Although Fundamental Consciousness is the fabric of the infinite universe, how do we experience it in our physical bodies?

The body holds three key centers through which we can perceive Fundamental Consciousness. Each center is a different portal to realizing a different quality of awakening. These energetic centers are called the *granthis*. In Sanskrit, *granthi* means "knot," or "tension." The body holds three main granthis:

- One is in the head.
- One is in the heart.
- One is in the belly.

As we come into our body more with presence and aware-ness, these granthis start to relax. The tension unwinds. We feel and perceive greater spaciousness.

When Fundamental Consciousness is realized through each of the centers, your experiences take on different qualities. When it happens in the head, you find clarity and contentment. Thinking stops or relaxes and you're just present. The mariachi band, as Jenny described it, stops for a moment and there's just open clarity.

When it happens in the heart, as Justin experienced, your heart opens up to love. You feel your seamless connec-tion with everyone and everything. You sense that you're not separate, that you belong to life. You might feel strange, surprisingly connected to someone you see on the news or on the street. You don't know them, but you feel this innate connection to them, even if they're from a different side of the political spectrum, a different religion, or a different country. Your heart has opened into this field of connec-tion. You honor them as part of creation.

It doesn't mean that you suddenly agree with their views, but rather that you recognize you are both aspects of the divine, and that makes you connected to each other. You care about the animals and the plants, too, because you sense their innate value and belonging in the universe.

The heart awakening opens up a whole new field of relatedness to life. With the head awakening, you may still be a little disassociated from life. But once your heart opens, you're totally connected to everything. You want to make a difference, to relieve suffering for yourself and others. You feel others almost as if they're yourself.

When it happens in the belly, some people feel a physical landing in the ground of their Being. It brings a felt sense of being at home in oneself, a sense of deep security. You feel okay for no reason. You know that even when things happen that are uncomfortable, you will be okay. You start to have more confidence to *be* yourself, because you're completely seated *in* yourself.

Awakenings can be linear, moving from center to center, but people can also have multiple awakenings at once. Remember Jenny and her knots of tension? She experienced a spontaneous awakening in her head, when the mariachi band in her mind quieted, as well as a spontaneous awakening in her belly, where she settled more deeply into her body.

Some people experience a pronounced and very obvious awakening in each of the three centers, but for many people it's a more integrated opening all at once. In any case, you gain more space, more freedom, and more permission to be who you are. The human urge to be an achiever, to strive to get somewhere, is softened. You no longer have to achieve or get somewhere else to feel safe or to be worthy. You find a deep security and well-being right where you are.

Fundamental Consciousness and Self-Esteem

So many kids have self-esteem issues. We often teach them to build themselves up to feel okay. But I teach that self-esteem doesn't come from changing who you are. It comes from *knowing* who you are as Fundamental Consciousness. When you realize this sacred part of yourself, you have natural confidence. You know your own divinity. You understand that you're intimately connected to creation, and you're here to participate in and serve creation.

THE BOTH/AND OF SPIRIT AND MATTER

When people first learn to meditate, many of them do so by separating from their mind and body. That leaves them split, leading two separate lives. They can only find their spiritual life when they close their eyes and go away to find the infinite, timeless aspect of themselves. Then they come back into life and lose it.

It was true for me. I would do my yoga practice, lie in *Savasana*, open to the infinite, and feel a rush of connection. "This is great! This is beautiful!" I would think. But as soon as I opened my eyes, I lost it. I was stuck in an either/or mentality, but never both at once.

As my awakening deepened and I became more integrated, I opened into a paradoxical both/and experience. I could see and feel the physical world, and at the same time feel and sense myself as Spirit. I had a both/and experience of wholeness, and it allowed me to walk my awakening in my everyday life. This is the deeper version of embodiment, where awakening walks with you moment to moment in the midst of everyday life.

In embodied awakening you land in the paradox of life: You are both finite and you are infinite. There is no need to leave the mind behind or forget your emotions. You can experience thoughts, sensations, and emotions—AND be abiding in Fundamental Consciousness at the same time.

Realizing Fundamental Consciousness

How do you realize Fundamental Consciousness?

For some people, the realization of Fundamental Consciousness comes naturally and easily. For the rest of us, there are several different ways to enter into the currents of awakening. Three practices that can support our awakening journey are embodied meditation, gazing, and glimpsing background awareness.

Embodied Meditation

The first practice is embodied meditation, which I teach in my courses. It's a simple process that asks you to make contact with yourself. In essence, you take your gaze and turn it inward to notice and feel your breath and notice and feel your body. Then you relax and open into the infinite aspect of yourself.

Gazing

Another practice is gazing. When choosing this, you can gaze at

- Yourself in the mirror;
- Something in nature; or
- Someone else who is gazing at you.

Gazing in the mirror, as Justin did, is a simple way to begin at home.

When gazing in nature, you sit in a larger environment. In this practice, you gaze with your eyes open at animals, plants, or other objects from nature. You can gaze softly at a tree, the sky, the stars, anything you want to open to and connect with. When you gaze, you are simply being.

In the third way of gazing is mutual gazing—gazing with someone else. This is when you sit across from someone else and make eye contact. You're both gazing at each other, opening your hearts. You're both the gazer and the receiver.

Babies are great to practice gazing with because they're so good at gazing. It comes naturally to them. Rumi, a fourteenth-century mystic poet, gazed with his spiritual teacher, Shams. This practice became an important catalyst in Rumi's awakening journey.

Gazing is nourishing because it helps to put you into the field of Fundamental Consciousness. There's nothing you need to do. You're okay as you are. It's not an achievement-based practice—you're not doing, you're just being. And it's in this space of just being that you can relax enough to open and realize your essence as Fundamental Consciousness itself.

A lot of people think that in order to awaken, they have to do a lot, or learn a lot. But the way forward is just to be. Maybe you're sitting in nature and gazing at a tree, just being with the tree. Maybe you're sitting at Starbucks, and you look over at a little infant in a stroller and for just a moment, you're just being—gazing with the infant. You're both present with each other, for as long as you want, or until one of you looks away.

Let go of the mindset "This will get me somewhere else," and move to "What happens if I just allow myself to be?"

Glimpsing Background Awareness

Another method you can use is called Glimpsing Background Awareness. Instead of habitually having your attention glued to objects, you're ungluing and noticing the space.

For example, take a break from looking at this book or your computer screen. Instead, relax and open and notice the space in the room between all the objects. Once you find the space, you can start perceiving *from* the space, and you can open into the wholeness of creation.

Allow yourself to explore these practices over the course of your day. Over time, it will start to feel more natural.

When we wake up to the field of Fundamental Consciousness, we feel more connected to everyone and everything. That gives us the opportunity to explore mutuality, relating in a more satisfying way with other people.

Chapter 6

MUTUALITY

*In a real sense all life is interrelated. All men are caught
in an inescapable network of mutuality, tied in a single
garment of destiny. Whatever affects one directly affects
all indirectly.*—Martin Luther King Jr.

Rebirth

Embodied awakening gave me the courage to face things
I had been putting off, including a phone call I dreaded.
It was the last lead I had to find my biological mother. If I
called and they didn't know how to find her, I would have
to throw out my entire adoption file and give up. This was
it. My last hope.

Braced by newfound calm and courage, I made the
phone call. I had the space to hold my fear and uncertainty,
and know that I would be okay even if it didn't go the way
I wanted it to.

The decades of separation compressed in a few short
weeks, and when we finally met in person, I felt whole and
loved.

But a few months later, she called and spoke with a sadness and fear in her voice.

"I love you," she said, "but it's really hard for me to talk to you."

I felt a flood of tension and stayed quiet.

She continued. "Talking to you brings up a lot of memories of when I was in high school," she said, "and how people ostracized me after I gave birth and gave you up for adoption."

She said the feelings were too overwhelming. "It's too hard for me to be in contact with you," she said. "I don't want to see you anymore."

I was deeply sad and disappointed. I didn't want to lose her. But I also completely understood her point of view. As I listened to her on the phone, I could feel her terror from being teased at school, as well as her deep sadness and shame from a teen pregnancy. Her well-being wasn't separate from mine.

"I love you," I said. "I want to have a relationship with you. I completely understand where you're coming from, and I'll honor your wishes."

Months went by with no contact. I still felt disappointed, but when I opened into the infinite field of Fundamental Consciousness, into the field that connects all living things, I could still feel her. Even though we weren't in communication, not even by email, I was aware of her presence. In that we space, we still had an immutable connection.

I experienced a deep connection and knew I had to let her be as she was, rather than trying to make her be another way. This meant allowing my biological mother to feel what she felt, while also honoring my own feelings and allowing myself to feel what I was feeling.

What I experienced is called mutuality: the ability to hold the creative tension of two people's different points of views. It's not about giving up your view. It's not about trying to change another's view. It's about allowing both to coexist at the same time.

Learning to Relate

Mutuality doesn't always come naturally to us. As a species, we have spent a long time in the paradigm of separation. In this mindset, the other is separate from me. If I perceive them as weaker than I am, I try to dominate, subjugate, or control them. If I see them as stronger than I am, I give in to them to survive their domination, subjugation, and control. That dynamic creates power hierarchies that are toxic and harmful. It's leading to our mutual destruction as a species: the destruction of our planet, chaos between countries, and suffering in personal relationships.

Mutuality is an alternate way of relating to the other. I first heard the term from one of my spiritual teachers, Saniel Bonder. He explained mutuality as a way to perceive others as part of the giant web of life, instead of seeing others as separate from us. Instead we experience a seamless connectedness with everything in existence, including people, plants, the earth, the stars, and the cosmos itself. With mutuality, not only can we survive as a species on this planet, but we can thrive.

> We're all familiar with Martin Luther King Jr.'s "I Have a Dream" speech, but did you know he also spoke about human connection? In fact, he coined the term "mutuality" to describe the interconnectedness of life.

We each may have unique and different points of views. When we realize our mutuality, we know that even so, we are still connected through the unifying field of Fundamental Consciousnesses. Our uniqueness and unity coexist at the same time. Before awakening, we think we're separate and seek to overpower or give in to others. But in awakening, we allow ourselves to be as we are, feel as we feel, and have our own opinions while allowing others to do the same. If the relationship matters, we allow ourselves to stay in the discomfort of our unique views.

In a relationship between two people, mutuality is the idea that while I have inherent value and my views matter, you also have inherent value and your views matter. We are both important parts of the whole. We relate to each other as if we both matter and are a sacred part of creation. Our relationship becomes a source of creative connection rather than disconnection and suffering.

We're able to be in a larger field where we feel seen and heard and honored, and that allows us to grow in our own authenticity and vulnerability. It allows us to cultivate a deeper sense of compassion for others and a true capacity to hear and feel the other. Our willingness to stay in the discomfort and uncertainty of creative tension gives us access to new possibility.

We are able to wake up to the sacredness of all our relationships. We experience more care, listening, respect, and honor for others and for our larger divine self. The impact on others can also be transformational. When another person feels really seen, heard, and valued, their edges soften. They open in a whole new way of relating. The mutuality in our relationships even helps both people evolve to the next level of their own maturation.

Experiencing Conflict Through Mutuality

Humans generally have two habitual strategies for relating to people: (1) Sometimes we give in to, fawn upon, or acquiesce. This may happen particularly with certain authority figures. (2) Other times, we try to fight or dominate others, such as friends or family members. We try to win the fight and overpower them.

Mutuality is part of our divine connection to Fundamental Consciousness, but to reach it, we have to learn to look past the ego-driven paradigm we live in. The habit of being human is perceiving difference as a threat. But in mutuality, difference is a unique manifestation of the one divine consciousness.

The paradigm of separation sets up a field of either/or: *either* your view is right, *or* the other person's view is right. You can either surrender and accept their view, or assert your dominance and force them to accept yours. Either way, it's a win-lose situation. There is a sense of conquering. The person who gives in feels resentful, angry, unseen, and unheard.

Living from the mind in a paradigm of separation creates a sense of confusion over our identity. Beliefs are seen as "who we are" and another's conflicting point of view becomes viewed as a threat to survival. This activates a need to fight to be right. Winning a fight ends the conflict, but it doesn't create any connection, joy, or love. Over time, this erodes intimacy in relationships.

The person who overpowers in the relationship becomes more insensitive. They haven't heard or felt the other person, and they don't know how to relate. Meanwhile, the person who has been conquered feels resentful. They also feel that the conflict isn't completely resolved.

This is our problem as a species. We don't really know

how to come into the field of mutuality. We have these habits that we've inherited, these automatic responses that served us in the early days of human evolution, but now they harm us.

When you come from mutuality, you relate in a new way. You find permission to let go of fight or flight, and no longer try to dominate or give in to others. You understand that it's not about only "your view" or only "their view." It's something brand new, never seen before, never done before. It is the raw, vulnerable, messy field of intimacy, relating, and caring. You are flowing with the immediacy of life, not trying to control the outcome in a predetermined way, but trusting in the larger field of Being.

Practicing mutuality, choose someone you share a small conflict with, yet with whom you feel emotionally safe. If you're going to be vulnerable and share your truth, it's helpful if the person is receptive. Start small. In learning yoga, you start with downward-facing dog, not a handstand in the center of the room. This is exactly the same thing. Start speaking your truth with a friend, one you know will listen to you. When you're done sharing your truth, make space for them to share their point of view and listen to what they have to say.

You will start to reach a level of mutuality where you're able to engage with more ease, enjoyment, connection, and fulfillment. You'll come to trust that when difficulties come up, which they will, you know how to work through them with mutual respect, care, and honor. Mutuality is not necessary in all relationships, just the ones you value with the people who are important in your life.

When we learn to approach conflicts through the lens of mutuality, we find communication so much easier. When we feel heard by the other person, and we're able to hear them in return, and we can hold each other's perspectives with respect. Sometimes even with respectful conversation, there's no immediate way forward. So mutuality invites us to a next level superpower—being able to hold "an unresolvable" conflict, feeling the frustration, anger, or fear that it brings up without shutting down.

COMPROMISING IS NOT MUTUALITY

It's easy to think mutuality is a more complex version of compromise, but it isn't. Compromise means that both people give up a small amount of who they are and what they believe, in order to find common ground in the middle. While compromise is often a better solution than conflict, it's still in the separation model. Two people who refuse to see the other's point of view give up a little bit at a time until they can both be satisfied. They chip away at their opinions until they can coexist, instead of allowing their opinions to naturally coexist even when they are at odds.

Making Space for Listening

When you come into a larger field of mutuality and embrace multiple perspectives, it is impossible not to grow. It doesn't mean you will always, or even often, come to agree with another person. Instead, it means that you have enough space, that you're awake enough in Fundamental Consciousness, to host more than one perspective. You're no longer confined to the small space in your dualistic ego-based mind.

You can do this through a Listening Practice. We listen in our heads, hearts, and whole being.

We all begin with the head. We're in conflict, stuck listening to what's inside our own head. Even when we think we're hearing another person, we're filtering everything through our judgments and thoughts. To be more effective, we can become open and available to really hear what the other person is trying to say.

Listening with the heart, we open to feeling the other person with compassion. We want to hear them, so we're reaching out with our heart center. We're able to feel ourselves, but we're also feeling the other person. This brings a deeper level of intimacy.

In the third way of listening, with our whole being, we're listening with our heads, hearts, and entire being, which includes the field of Fundamental Consciousness.

We open up the lake of self so we can actually listen to

the words and the feelings at the same time, even if they're contradictory to our own words and feelings. We come into intimacy with the other person, existing in the same field. Even though we still have differences, we're in the same space. We feel more space and possibility for new solutions, arising from the larger field of mystery.

> ### ENTERING THE FIELD OF BEING
>
> Entering the field doesn't save you from feeling emotions. Like Kaliya, the sea monster in chapter 3, it gives you more space, both to feel your own feelings and to relate to the other person. On a human level I missed my biological mother, and I felt sad and disappointed and hurt. But I had space to feel that without being overwhelmed because I could enter the field of Being.

Allowing for Miracles

The mystery of mutuality means we never really know what's going to happen. We cannot control or predict outcomes, because we are allowing the process to unfold.

Sometimes, what unfolds is miraculous.

About a year after my biological mother said she no longer wanted to hear from me, I got an email from her.

"I miss you," she wrote. "I'm wondering if you want to try again with this relationship."

I was thrilled, and I knew that outcome was only possible because I had listened to her, and then vulnerably shared how disappointed and sad I was.

When she wanted to end our relationship, I could have reacted and run away, and it would have been understandable. I could have argued or bargained with her to get what I wanted. I could have used my hurt to guilt her into changing her mind.

But because I sank into my heart center and entered into whole-being listening, I was able to hold her view with respect. And because I had the courage to share my view, it gave her the opportunity to hear it and respect it too. That opened a path for reconciliation that wouldn't have been possible otherwise. We each held what was unresolvable—until she was ready to reconnect.

Miracles are not guaranteed. You can never know what outcome your interactions may have. But when you practice mutuality, you cultivate a field of possibility.

Listening to Yourself

We often think we're listening to others, when really we're listening to our own thoughts. We're so busy processing our thoughts and judgments, we don't truly hear what the other person is actually saying. Through mutuality, the interconnectedness in the field of open availability and curiosity, we become able to hear others.

But sometimes when we first learn to listen to other people, we stop listening to ourselves. That leads to resentment in relationships, because we're so over there on their side that we've lost contact with ourselves: with our own truth, our own values, and our own voice.

With mutuality, we're able to listen to others while listening to ourselves at the same time. This means honoring our own feelings, perspectives, and truths, while honoring the other person's truths. In the mutuality, we're ultimately engaging in whole-being listening.

In embodied awakening, the obstacles become part of the path. Let's see how to include roadblocks in the overall field of consciousness.

Chapter 7

CHALLENGES AS PATH

Let life happen to you. Life is always in the right.
—Rainer Maria Rilke

Blessing the Studio

When I opened my own studio, my yoga teacher, Tim Miller, gave me a beautiful Ganesha statue. Ganesha is a Hindu deity, a mythological elephant god. I learned that Ganesha was the "remover of obstacles" and the "lord of new beginnings." By removing challenges, the elephant god gave you good luck.

In other traditions, people might give you a four-leaf clover, or they might give you a lucky rabbit's foot. In yogic tradition, they give you a statue of Ganesha. It was a blessing for the opening of my studio, Yoga Del Mar, and I was incredibly touched.

Soon after, I traveled to Thailand, and I bought a stunning two-foot-tall wood carving of Ganesha to hang on the wall in the studio. Seeing the wood carving, several friends over the years gifted me with Ganeshas, and my collection grew. I was thrilled. I thought, *"Wow, I'm really going to have a lot of obstacles removed!"*

A few years after I opened the studio, one of my other yoga teachers told me that Ganesha is both the bringer and the remover of obstacles. I was floored. "Do I need to get rid of my Ganesha collection?" I worried, thinking maybe I was bringing strife into my life.

My teacher laughed. "I guess it depends on what you want from life. Do you want it to be easy, or do you want to grow?" He explained that as part of the divine unfoldment of life, Ganesha brings these obstacles in order to provide you with growth. Once you've grown, gotten the lesson, learned, and woken up, those obstacles are naturally removed. The obstacles are path. They're the way forward, to help you grow in the precise direction you need.

I realized my collection was exactly what I wanted and needed: a life that would help me always grow and evolve. Challenges are an inherent part of life, not punishment for doing something wrong. They help you grow to the next level of your humanity. It's a natural part of your awakening journey. By embracing and honoring your challenges, you expand more into the totality of your being. Challenges help you become more competent, skilled, and whole. They are not a mistake. They are part of your divine path.

Walking Through Obstacles

When we face challenges in life, the mind has a habit of saying something like, "This shouldn't be happening, this is wrong, why is this happening to me?" We want the person causing the obstacle to be different. We want life to be different. We even want ourselves to be different. We carry a victim mentality that constantly believes, "Life is doing this thing to me."

But this is a habit of separation. Because we believe we are separate from life, we think what's happening shouldn't be happening. We go into the fight, flight, or freeze mode: we try to avoid the challenge, we try to manipulate it and force it to change, or we freeze and shut down.

"Obstacle as path," or "what's in the way is the way," is a next level perspective on our habit of separation. When we realize that everything is one, our obstacles become part of our lives. They are part of the natural unfoldment of life.

When you can't embrace your obstacles as path, you feel stuck. You might even feel anxious, depressed, empty, or frustrated. You see life as a conveyor belt, and anything unexpected trips you up, clogs the gears in the machine. You end up feeling small, stuck, and separate from life. You suffer unnecessarily, and worst of all, the challenge is still there. You can't grow from it because you aren't meeting it openly—you aren't including it and relating to it honestly—and you don't trust that it will lead you into your next iteration, your next developmental stage.

When you acknowledge obstacle as path, on the other hand, you realize, "Life is *for* me, and this challenge here in front of me is *for* my growth and development. I might not like it. It might be uncomfortable, it might be messy, but it is here to show me where I'm not able to stay present, how I'm lacking the skills and competency to move through this particular situation." In essence, your obstacles and challenges show you precisely where the edges of your awakening or the edges of your maturation are—and help you continue to grow

When you embrace obstacles as path you wake up. You are now in Presence. You start to clearly see and feel the challenge, and become intimately engaged with your life again. The resistance softens, and the habitual need to fight the obstacle and make it different relaxes. Instead, you open into a field of mutuality with the challenge itself and begin to listen to what life is asking of you: How are you being invited to grow?

Waking Up to Challenge

To embrace a challenge, greet it like a new friend. Specifically, take a moment to slow down. Get curious. Notice what's going on in your physical, emotional, and mental bodies. How does your body feel? What are your emotions?

What is your mind saying? The real challenge is what's going on inside you—and what you don't know how to be with.

This is an opportunity to explore deeper within. This practice is Waking Up in the Midst of Challenge. During this practice, we identify where we have difficulty being with a feeling. For example:

- I'm feeling angry.
- I'm feeling scared.
- I'm feeling sad.
- I'm feeling insecure.
- I'm feeling anxious.

When you feel these things, give yourself permission to be as you are. Notice the tendency to try to push or force yourself to feel something different. Instead, allow yourself to be as you are. Allow yourself to get curious about the situation. Pause and let yourself feel what you feel. Go deeper into the moment and find the space within to sit with that uncomfortable feeling.

For most people, the habit when facing a challenge is, "Let me go up to my head to figure out how to solve this." Or, "Let me call a friend to feel better." Instead, the invitation in Embodied Awakening is, "Can I drop into my body, and can I feel what's going on with me? Can I slow down and feel?"

The head often wants to solve the problem. But

frequently that turns into fixing and avoiding, rather than feeling the discomfort. Blaming someone else for the challenge is another way to distract yourself from your own feelings Again, the invitation is to feel into your body and discover how this challenge is inviting *you* to grow.

Allowing yourself to be honest, real, and vulnerable can soften the defensive positions of the mind. It drops you into a deeper courageous intimacy with the moment precisely as it is. When you become engaged, curious, and available, the solutions naturally arise from the mystery of being. Instead of just getting by, or getting through, you are powerfully changed by your whole-hearted participation.

CHALLENGE VS. DANGER

Challenges are distinct from danger. If you're in danger, that is immediate and means something needs to happen right away. If a rattlesnake writhes in my living room, I'm not going to feel into it. That's exactly the kind of situation that fight or flight was designed to help us survive! The problem is when you fall into fight or flight in response to a challenge rather than a danger. You may solve the problem, but you won't evolve. If you do face danger, it's good to process your emotions after the fact—just not while the rattlesnake is still rattling.

Radical Self-Care

Radical self-care is another practice along the path. This is especially important when experiencing challenges.

Often people think that self-care is selfish. That simply isn't true. Your awakening contributes to everybody around you. It's how you show up for your partner, kids, family, friends, and community. It reverberates out into the world. It's really one of the most generous things you can do.

Even if self-care is a regular part of your routine, many people find they need a lot more self-care than they did previously as they begin to awaken. As you deepen into being with your emotions, and develop a raw, vulnerable intimacy with yourself and others, it can shake up a lot inside. So it's important to know how to resource yourself.

Here are some resourcing techniques:

- **Sensing.** Take a moment to sense what feels good in your body. Use that as a resource while also including parts of your body that might be uncomfortable. See if you can feel both at the same time.

- **Grounding.** Feel your feet on the ground or your hips on the chair right now. Or go for a walk and feel your feet in the dirt. Let the energy flow through you and connect to the ground. If you don't have a safe space to take your shoes off and walk on the earth, touch the plants as you walk and feel their leaves against your skin.

- **Breathing.** Learn to connect to your breath to regulate your nervous system. One way of doing this is box breathing: Inhale to a count of five, hold for a count of five, exhale to a count of five, and then hold for a count of five. Repeat this five or six times.

- **Being in nature.** Go out in nature and allow yourself to be nourished by sunlight and the trees. The natural world can be a really powerful resource on the journey of awakening.

- **Moving.** For many people, being able to move their bodies helps move the energy and feels nurturing. This is true whether it's a gentle practice like Tai Chi or yoga, or it's exercise like going for a walk, going to the gym, or dancing.

- **Connecting.** A huge source of nourishment and self-care can be connecting with other people. Call a friend that you know will be able to listen to you, and perhaps say, "I'm having a lot of difficulty right now. Could you just listen to me for five minutes?" Reaching out socially like that can be incredibly helpful, whether to a friend or a family member.

- **Eating healthy foods.** You want to make sure your body is nourished on a physical level with alive, whole foods. Less-processed foods are more nourishing and can really be helpful, as is drinking a lot of water.

- **Joining an awakening group.** As we discuss later on in the community chapter, having a group of others who are on the same journey can be a helpful part of self-care.

Awakening is almost like being pregnant: you're in a deep, transformational process. No one questions that you should take care of yourself when you're growing a baby! So don't hesitate to take care of yourself as you grow into the next phase of your development. Give yourself support, care, and nourishment. And be open to receive it from others as well.

RESOURCING WITH OTHERS

Awakening doesn't mean we have to do it alone. When we're going through challenges, we can lean into and resource from our community. Consider going for a walk with a mate or friend and just being quietly there for each other.

Healing Through Obstacles

Sometimes, the possibilities that open to us are windows into ourselves.

That was the case for Marnie, a woman in her seventies who worked with me on her path of awakening. As she got more in touch with her feelings and began to recognize challenges as opportunities, she started to realize that she was still harboring a lot of childhood hurt. She was a middle child, and she felt that she had never been seen or understood by her mom, Ruth. As a child, she often fought with her sisters, and the older one picked on her mercilessly, but her mother did not step in to protect her.

Marnie was shocked to realize how sad and angry she still was about how she had been treated as a child. It had been so many years ago, and she thought she was over it as she focused on her career, marriage, and family. But as she began to awaken, the unresolved challenges came to the forefront.

When Marnie chatted with her mother, Ruth, now in her nineties, they rarely spoke about anything serious. In fact, it was hard for Marnie to get a word in at all. Ruth would talk and talk, but she wouldn't listen. So Marnie decided to be courageous. On one call, Marnie asked, "Can I have five minutes of uninterrupted time while you just listen to me?"

Her mother was surprised, but agreed. Marnie shared

that she realized she was still harboring some anger and hurt from childhood, all those long years ago, about feeling unseen and unloved. She knew it was her story she was telling herself, but she wanted her mom to know.

Finally, Marnie asked, "Why is it that you never stood up for me in the conflicts with my older sister?"

"I didn't know how," her mom admitted.

Those simple words unleashed a flood of kindness in Marnie, both toward her mother and toward herself. She saw that Ruth wasn't intentionally trying to be mean to her. She realized that her mother's way of dealing with things was not dealing with them, avoiding them. Because she didn't know how to address something, she didn't address it at all. That conversation was a huge turning point in their relationship. Marnie saw Ruth as she was, instead of judging her through the lens of her own childhood thoughts.

Marnie's obstacle turned into an opportunity for growth. It was a miracle. As time passed, they started having deeper, more soulful conversations. Marnie was vulnerable and authentic and shared deeply with her mom, and Ruth was able to become more open and receptive.

It may seem amazing that anger can be the birthplace of intimacy. But when Marnie expressed her feelings of hurt, confusion, and anger, the very challenge became the path forward into greater intimacy, care, connection, love, and healing. In this way, challenges help us learn, grow, and heal.

Often, the biggest challenges we face are unconscious. Sometimes, these obstacles are the unfelt, repressed hurts from childhood that we store deep in our bodies, emotions, and psyche. As we'll see, healing trauma is also part of the path for finding greater freedom, ease, and well-being.

Chapter 8

TRAUMA

Trauma is not what happens to you; trauma is what happens inside you as a result of what happens to you.—Gabor Maté, MD

Healing Generational Patterns

Susan grew up in a very traditional family, where the males were valued over the females. Although Susan was brilliant, talented, and more accomplished than her brother, he was prioritized over her. She was conditioned to stand in the background of the family. Her mother also took on this cultural role of serving her husband and son. They took priority over herself.

As an adult, Susan wanted to live in a different way. She went to college, got an advanced degree, and raised her children to feel equally valued.

But when Susan talked to her mother on the phone, she noticed herself falling back into those old family patterns. It seemed that her mother only called when she wanted

Susan to do something for other family members. Talking to her mother, Susan felt trapped by the old patterns, and she started to feel intense anger and resentment.

Susan believed that her parents only valued her for what she could do to serve her mother, father, and brother, rather than for who she was herself.

After working with me in the awakening group, Susan was able to stand up for herself, ask for what she needed, and set healthy boundaries. When Susan allowed herself to feel the anger, she released the trauma pattern and had the freedom to take on new behaviors. She stopped waiting for her family to change and value her. She began to value herself and her worth as a woman, independent of her family of origin.

Susan's experience stems from ancestral trauma. The hurt she felt as a child was a generational wound of shame, unworthiness, and neglect passed down from her ancestors. Susan's shift set in motion a new family pattern and new possible future for her daughter.

Bringing Awareness to Trauma

Trauma is unfelt emotions that are trapped in the body, whether you are aware of them or not. It happened in the past, and it overwhelmed your system. That resulted in your system closing down, shutting out that piece of information and blocking it off. But the information is still in your body, and it's still impacting you in each moment. It shapes the patterns of your life.

Trauma is the repressed feelings inside us. Every day, we are using our energy to keep those painful feelings out of our awareness so we don't experience them. We might not be aware of what we're doing. For instance, we might have an instant of fear, and then push it below the surface.

When you have trauma, it means you experienced something that overwhelmed your nervous system, and you couldn't fully process it, so you stopped the emotion entirely. Trauma is not the event, but the way our nervous system created compensatory patterns.

Maybe you lost a parent and instead of being able to grieve, you had to go back to work. Maybe you were teased and bullied as a kid, and you didn't want to feel embarrassed because that triggered even more teasing, so you stopped feeling. Maybe you hate your job, but you don't think you have the right to feel angry so you bury it deep inside. Whatever the incident is, trauma happens when you stop the feeling from being felt. You take that energy, that unfelt emotion, and you store it in your body. It doesn't have a chance to go to completion, to unwind, so its energy can release and find freedom.

Often these unfinished elements from our past happened during childhood, when we didn't have a mature nervous system that could process what we were going through. As children, we needed someone with an attuned nervous system to help us process our sadness, fear, anger, etc., but often we grew up in homes where our parents were unable to meet us in our pain. So we stored it in our bodies, but eventually, we reach a point where we are ready to release that pain and trauma to find healing.

Our bodies can hold three general kinds of trauma:

- Personal
- Cultural
- Ancestral

Personal trauma is something that happened to you, in this lifetime, that was overwhelming or too much for your nervous system to process at the time. You may or may not consciously remember the event, but it's stored in your body.

Cultural trauma has a broader scope. We are born into a culture, in a specific time period with specific general events. When we come in into the world, we're coming in through the unfinished past of our culture and country. Those of us born in the United States are dealing with the trauma of racism, political issues, environmental degradation, and dominator societies, just to name a few. In the wider scope of humanity, the conflict between the feminine and the masculine is a universal cultural trauma that impacts us. These issues in the world live inside as well. We aren't separate from them.

Finally, ancestral trauma also affects us. Just as we inherit great traits from our ancestors, like our intelligence, physical health, or musical interests, we also inherit their unfinished pasts. We inherit the unprocessed feelings they were not able to heal. Think of a woman who sacrifices her life in order to support her children and her husband. That sense of sacrifice can be passed down generation after generation.

Repressing Feelings

Repressing our uncomfortable feelings takes energy. Every moment of the day, we hold this information out of our awareness. Imagine there's a wall that's about to fall on us, and we don't want it to fall. So we try holding the wall up, whispering, "Don't fall, don't fall." Trauma is like that. We hold it at bay and whisper, "Don't feel, don't feel. Don't know." That avoidance drains our energy and attention. It creates a consciousness of separation as we direct the energy into the mind, instead of allowing our awareness to distribute evenly throughout our whole being.

Emotions are energy. When you feel the painful feelings, you liberate the energy of the feelings themselves. That energy is restored to your system. You also liberate the energy you were using to keep those feelings frozen and unfelt. Releasing it all returns the energy to the natural flow of your being.

> ## THE PHYSICAL RESULT OF TRAUMA
>
> Often, trauma is literally felt in the body. It may show up as a frozen shoulder, a disease, or an imbalance in your digestive system. When we meet these areas and come into relationship with the feelings that we weren't able to feel when we were younger, it creates flow, which allows for presence. It allows for a greater felt sense of our wholeness to begin to emerge.

Surrendering to the Process

When intentionally healing the trauma, you learn to surrender to the process and allow the feelings to be felt. Once those feelings come up, you can't ignore them.

If my unfelt sadness came up before awakening, before I started to become more sensitive, I had all kinds of strategies for pushing it back down and not feeling. But part of what happens in awakening is that you no longer have the ability to not feel. You are too open and too aware, and you can't so easily push things away. It becomes more painful not to deal with them, and harder to push them back down.

Exhaustion is also a factor. It takes a lot of energy to keep everything out of awareness, and it takes a toll on you. Often, by the time people get into their awakening journey, they're exhausted from running away from themselves.

There's a surrender into the process. I'll describe this more when I talk about the core ache of separation in the next chapter, but essentially, it means coming to the point where you realize that fighting or running from this pain isn't any easier or less painful than meeting it head on.

At the same time, a strange and beautiful thing happens. You recognize that these feelings are the gateway to your greater freedom, and you no longer *want* to push them back down again. It's still uncomfortable to face your trauma and shadows. Part of you probably wants to escape in any way you can, but another part of you realizes this is a valuable part of the journey. If you don't experience it, you don't grow. You stay stuck, and don't get to evolve and keep going.

You begin to reach out for opportunities to process and heal. You become a willing participant in the process. But go easy on yourself. You may need time to experience layers of feelings. Depending on the intensity of your feelings, you may also want to engage professional support to work through the journey.

Releasing Trauma

Trauma is an extension of cause and effect. Like Newton's third law of motion, for every action there's an equal and opposite reaction. Trauma is the residue in your nervous system of unprocessed emotions from the past. When you hold that tension to not feel, to stay safe, it starts to impact your body. You're missing part of your wholeness. You start to feel incomplete in your system.

When uncomfortable feelings come up, we revert to fight, flight, or freeze and intensify the feeling of living in separation. Trauma is an unhealed wound and missed connection to ourselves and others. We can heal that wound by feeling what we were unable to feel in the past and letting our energy flow freely again.

Bringing New Opportunities

There's no need to go hunting for ways to complete your trauma. Life will always give you opportunities to do so. If there's embarrassment that you never felt, you're going to find yourself in all these situations that bring up this feeling of embarrassment. If you never processed your grief, you'll see examples of grief and loss all around you. It's like the unfinished past wants to complete itself, so you can find greater freedom.

That isn't to say this process is easy. If it was, you would have done it a long time ago. Be on the lookout for these opportunities, and make sure that you're ready to comfort yourself and heal as you process these big, thorny emotions. Have another person there to hold you and feel with you. Let yourself break down and cry as you feel the full extent of your honest feelings.

When you do, it's like going through a tunnel of transformation. All the tangled energy that you've been holding in your body releases into a free flow of life. Your body feels better, because you're no longer expending so much energy to hold that emotion down. You may feel a physical release of tension in your body, in your hips or your shoulders or your chest. With this new part integrated back into the wholeness, you will feel more alive, more vibrant, and more able to make new choices. You will naturally open into new directions.

Every time you go through this process of feeling and digesting your emotions, you unleash your natural energy flow and open up a little more access to Fundamental Consciousness. You will have more space and feel more grounded in yourself, which will give you greater competency and capacity to meet whatever arises next in your healing and awakening journey. You'll be able to open deeper karmic blocks. Once you go through this tunnel of transformation, you will feel much better on the other side—more whole, more grounded, more spacious, more relaxed, and more like yourself.

Healing Our Connected Past

> ### THE LUXURY OF HEALING
>
> In many ways, we are the first generation that has the luxury—the time, the energy, the resources—to process our unprocessed feelings from the past. Our ancestors were so busy surviving, that it was basically all they could do. They didn't have energy to sit down and process their trauma. For the most part, it was just "get through the day, put food on the table, and do it all again tomorrow." But modern technology has taken away a lot of the burden of survival, and we now have the space to actually process the unprocessed past and create new levels of freedom for ourselves.

When you process and feel and heal trauma—whether personal, cultural, or ancestral—the healing capacity uploads into humanity as a whole. It benefits everyone. You start out doing it for yourself, because here it is in your life and in your body. But we are all interconnected, so the work you do individually impacts everyone. Your healing work will more directly impact the people in your immediate circle—your beloved partner, your children, and your close friends—but it reverberates further out, rippling into the world.

When you do your work on the path of awakening, it's going out into the world in current time, and of course, it's moving into the future, because you're no longer leaving a legacy of trauma for your offspring to process. You've created new movement for life that the next generation will inherit. But according to the shamanic traditions, your healing impacts seven generations before you, as well as seven generations after you. You're actually sending healing through the generations.

Healing cultural trauma also contributes to improving the larger fabric of culture. We live in a culture full of traumatized people. It is the air we breathe. It shows up in the way our institutions function in a fragmented and polarized way. It shows up in the way we treat the earth, raping and pillaging her resources. Healing our trauma allows us to heal the fabric of society and birth a new culture and new world.

All the trauma we heal prepares us for perhaps the greatest pain inside—something I call the core ache of separation.

Chapter 9

THE CORE ACHE OF SEPARATION

So many of us have a belief that we were born unworthy, inadequate, unlovable, and alone.—Adyashanti

Falling into the Dark

No matter how successful we are, we reach a point in our lives when we long for more at our core.

Carol was a highly driven, very successful professional. As she began her awakening journey, she started to long for something more. She realized that she had been driven her whole life by an underlying ache of separation, a gnawing emptiness, sadness, and sense that there must be something more to life. She thought that the next degree or achievement would save her from that discomfort, but instead she felt increasingly untethered and disoriented.

Carol lost interest in those around her, even her closest friends and family. She began to pull away, directing her attention and energy to hunting for something to give her a sense of connection, of purpose. She thought that she was searching for meaning.

Working with her, I helped her realize the truth was that she was running away from the uncomfortable feelings inside.

When Carol came fully into awakening, she relaxed and settled down into herself—right through those dark and complex emotions—and opened into her infinite nature. She saw that she had been seeking meaning externally instead of looking for it within. By connecting with herself, she finally learned who she was, and realized that she loved working with kids and teaching school.

Carol changed careers and started working as a school teacher. Her new career brought her deep fulfillment for many years. She reconnected with friends and family, and found the fullness of herself.

Facing the core ache of separation that exists within us all is the crux of embodied awakening. This ache, with its layers of grief, shame, fear and longing, can be painful to confront, but when we allow ourselves to move through it, we begin to see the truth of ourselves. We come to understand that we are both finite and infinite, both human and divine. In embracing this paradox, we discover our ability to connect deeply with life and everything around us.

Acknowledging the Core Ache of Separation

A core feeling of discomfort exists within all of us, and it is there throughout our lives. Adyashanti called it the core wound of unworthiness. I call it the core ache of separation, because it is the fundamental pain of human existence when living in separation from our spiritual wholeness.

The core ache of separation is the place where our finite nature—our humanness—intersects with our infinite nature, our timelessness. It is the nexus between "I'm human," and "I'm divine—I'm something more."

The core ache of separation comes as a byproduct of our ego development. In chapter 2, we discussed the development of ego that happens around age two. Ego gives us a separate sense of self, which is a beautiful and important part of our growth. Striving in the material world teaches us to look at our relationship to the world in a physical way, and we need that learning. But it's also painful. We lose our connection to the infinite when we start to feel more separate and individual.

That pain gets driven down and becomes an unconscious motivation to push even harder. We think: "I'm separate from everybody. I have to achieve. I have to make something of myself." We go forward in life, the pain driving us to get the next degree, to reach the next achievement, to accomplish the next thing.

And then, sometimes suddenly, we reach that point

when striving for material success, or striving for even more success than we've already attained, is no longer satisfying. We're exhausted by the push to keep striving, and that exhaustion leads us inward. This slowing down and turning inward allows us to make deeper contact with ourselves. We often begin to feel what's underneath—the ache of separation that has propelled our outward journey in life and is the source of our discomfort.

We often feel the ache in the body, as a tension in the diaphragm or at the base of the sternum, or as a pain in the belly. When that happens, the contrast between our finite and infinite selves begins to feel uncomfortable. It sometimes feels like we're trapped in our skin while sensing that we're actually something more. It is that dissatisfaction, that growing awareness of the core ache of separation, that's a sign of our readiness for the awakening journey.

Dissecting the Core Ache

The core ache of separation is experienced in three main ways:

- A sense of unworthiness
- A longing for union
- A feeling of never doing enough

The first, which the yogic tradition calls *anava mala*, is a feeling of unworthiness. When confronted with anava mala, most people allow the ache of unworthiness to become a propellant in their life. Like Carol, they run away from that discomfort. They look for solutions. "If I got a better job I'd feel better. If I got a better mate, I'd feel better."

The second feeling is called *maiya mala*, a longing for union and connection. Often people enter into embodied awakening when they start to see that it's painful to be separate from themselves, separate from other people, and separate from the world. One of my students, Taylor, said she felt like she was living behind a sheet of plexiglass. Even when she was around other people, she felt separate and alone.

My client Martin encountered maiya mala at the park with his granddaughter, who was six years old. He noticed that she looked really sad, so he went and sat next to her. "What's wrong?" he asked.

"Pap, I feel very lonely," she told him.

"It's okay, honey. I'm right here," he said.

She looked at him and said, "I know, I just feel very lonely."

Martin, who loved her deeply, sat right in front of her, but she still felt separate and alone. Even at six years old, she felt maiya mala.

When you really get in touch with how painful it is to be living a life in separation, maiya mala leads you to long for something more. You begin to long to know the more infinite part of yourself, and you long for union and connection.

The third and final aspect of this core ache of separation is a feeling of never doing enough; of inadequacy, *or karma mala*. Have you heard the expression "the hamster wheel of life"? Sometimes life can feel like an endless struggle to reach a destination you never arrive at. That feeling of karma mala leaves you struggling to attain, to be enough. You feel unable to take action that has any meaning. You long for more ease and flow.

When you're ready for awakening, living as a limited human being becomes difficult. These feelings of unworthiness, loneliness, and inadequacy are not a sign of failure. They don't mean that there's anything wrong with you. They are, in fact, the opposite—the precursor to your spiritual awakening and a signpost that you're ready.

Learning to Read the Signs

After reading a post I had written about the core ache of separation, my student Shanti told me, "Your post helped shift my perspective about these unsettling feelings of longing, of yearning, of never being satisfied, of never being enough. I saw that they always represented in my mind and heart what was wrong with me. That post made me feel, even if just for a minute, that these feelings might be what's right with me."

Like many people, you may feel lost when you first begin to confront the core ache of separation. You might feel scared and overwhelmed. You may think there is something wrong with you for struggling. You may feel guilty—if life is so wonderful, why can't I just be happy? You may feel like Don in chapter 2, on his deathbed realizing he had no idea who he truly was. To the logical mind, this paradox can be confusing: you have a great life, but also feel like something is missing or wrong at the core of your being.

Dropping into the ache of separation can make you feel like you're failing. The striving of your first life has subsided, and you feel uncomfortable. It sometimes feels like a nagging, sinking feeling of inadequacy that brings with it the self-deflating thought, "I'm not enough."

A common instinct to escape that guilt and shame is to engage in material and sensory experiences. People do this in ways that may be extreme and uncharacteristic for them, such as buying luxury cars, having marital affairs, or going on exotic trips. If you are falling into these patterns of avoidance, try to avoid blaming yourself. Acknowledge the cycle you're in, and try to surrender to the ache of the moment instead of escaping from it. There's something for you in this discomfort, this core tension.

This isn't a mistake in your journey. You're not doing it wrong. This is a sacred threshold.

The longing is there to guide you home. It is a sacred invitation to open back up into your wholeness, beyond the exclusivity of knowing only the world of separation.

Falling into the Ache

When you begin to feel the core ache of separation, it helps to think of it as a door that has opened in front of you. You have an opportunity, and it's up to you whether you fight it or embrace it.

When you encounter that ache, you can surrender into the ache of the moment, the tension of it. Fall into it. Your path forward is to cooperate with the process. Instead of struggling, relax into the pain and the discomfort.

Struggling to get out of it creates discomfort and anxiety. Struggling to get it to go away leads to anger and frustration. You can do all that, but ultimately, the ache is still there, waiting for you to feel it. Resistance is futile.

Surrendering the struggle and cooperating with the intelligence of the journey lets you relax through this discomfort into your own infinite nature. You live in tandem with everyday life, and find and recognize your connection to it. At the bottom of the quicksand, you discover a secret portal to the infinite, a threshold you can embrace.

You can learn to fall into the ache of separation by finding the moments where it arises in the midst of your everyday life.

Say you're at a party, surrounded by friends and family members, when you start to feel lonely. Instead of trying to cheer yourself up or make yourself connect to everybody, why not allow yourself to recognize that you're going through this particular stage? Acknowledge that right now, you feel disconnected from people, and you feel lonely. You don't have to try to fix or change yourself. The only thing you can do is allow yourself to feel. As you allow the feeling to be, it can start to release. The tension can begin to move. You give yourself permission to feel lonely when you feel lonely.

Or what if you achieve something that should be wonderful, but it's not fulfilling on a deep level? Maybe you get a promotion at work, one you've been working toward forever, but it feels empty, hollow. Give yourself space to feel that sense of anticlimactic disappointment. Maybe you would have felt a thrill in the past, but now the thrill isn't there.

The mind tells you, "This feeling could go on forever." It's no wonder you're afraid of the future. But all you can know for sure is that this sense of hollowness, loneliness, and disappointment is here right now. To counteract the fear and pain, remind yourself that the ache is already there, in your chest. You're already feeling lonely or dissatisfied. Struggling against it doesn't make that feeling go away, it just hides it for a moment.

Relaxing into it, facing it with loving awareness, self-compassion, and resourcing is the only way to really move through it.

This is the passage into embodied awakening. Everything we've covered in the previous chapters prepares you for this, the actual passage into embodied awakening. With support and guidance, as you learn to allow yourself to feel this core ache of separation, it relaxes. The core ache of separation is a portal into awakening into your infinite, timeless, eternal sense of self that is content and connected to all that is.

THE CYCLE IS ENDLESS

The awakening journey in a sense is endless. We continue to go through different iterations of awakening. Right now, you may be focused on the big transition into embodiment and awakening to spirit, but there are more turns of the cycle. You are in the process of ongoing spiritual development. Don't be alarmed if you feel that core ache of separation even after awakening as you continue to integrate.

Letting Grace Lead You

As you walk this path toward your timeless, infinite self, I invite you to open up and appreciate the grace of the universe that guides you along.

Grace is a natural, benevolent force that's helping to unfold our evolutionary awakening journey. Sometimes grace is gentle and guides us to, say, pick up a book that's helpful for us and read it. Sometimes grace is fierce, like when we're falling to our knees in pain or sadness over a loss in life, and we have no idea what's next. Grace is a force that's always supporting us in our awakening journey.

Part of the awakening journey is recognizing that unlike all the other successes you've had in life, where it's been up to you to make it happen, awakening is a natural process of human development. It's guided and led by the winds of grace. Instead of trying to control it, you're invited to cooperate and surrender.

Align with grace, align with the winds of life as they're coming, and you will feel a deeper intimacy with yourself, with life, and with all that is. Next, you will learn how to continue that process of awake living every day.

Chapter 10

AWAKE LIVING

One with the earth, with the sky. One with everything in life.—Kenny Loggins

Living with Awakening

One of my clients had a young child who said to her one day, "Mom, do you know you're nothing and everything?"

My client was amazed. At just seven years old, her son had put into words exactly what she was beginning to learn.

"Yes, honey, I do," she told him. "Do *you* experience that you're nothing and everything at the same time?"

"Yes," he said. "Do you?"

"I don't always remember it," this young mother said, "But yes, a lot of the time, I know that too."

This is awakening. Understanding that we are "nothing"—and we are "everything"—all of creation and infinite consciousness.

When you wake up to this oneness of creation, you live every day connected to everyone and everything.

Changing Every Day

Awake living informs and changes your humanity. You develop more compassion for other people because you have more space in which to hold them. You have more choice in how you respond to outside stimuli.

Before you're awake, you don't feel okay, and you start to depend on outside interactions going well in order to bring that sense of rightness and success. If you're with a person who has a different view than yours, politically or religiously, for instance, it's so easy to fall into that "I've got to be right, and you've got to be wrong" mentality. Or maybe the other person is more powerful, a boss or a parent, so you put your own opinion aside to accept theirs, but you feel a sense of loss and failure as you do.

When you wake up to realizing Fundamental Consciousness, the infinite timeless aspect of yourself while you're also in your body, that whole interaction changes. You have more space, and you can hold both views at the same time. You can speak your truth without being confrontational, because you're resting in a part of yourself that's already okay. You're grounded and connected—both awake and divine: both/and. You are living in full humanity and living in divinity at the same time.

Because of that, you can engage more in the mystery and appreciate how the other person is different from you. You find beauty in that. You can allow your feelings as well as another's to be there, because you are connected to the okayness of your infinite nature. That's the game changer, the secret sauce that makes awake living so powerful and turns it into a catalyst for true evolution. You emerge into your next level of humanity and start to bring something new to the planet, instead of just rehashing those old patterns of conflict that have been here for thousands of years.

Embodied spiritual awakening isn't just about having a singular experience of awakening—although those momentary realizations, shifts, and changes are important. It's about living your awakening—moment to moment—as you walk in life. It's an ongoing, ever-changing awareness that will continue to expand, growing and shifting as you live your life. I call this *awake living*.

Within this constant evolution, there are different stages, depending on the realizations that have brought you to that point. Each stage creates a new way of perceiving life, of engaging life, of being in life.

WALKING FOREVER

The term "walking forever" comes from the work of Thomas Hübl, one of my teachers. He explains that our embodied awakening is something we're forever unfolding in our life. We're never done with this journey. It's not like we graduate and we're done. The integration of our awakening into our life is ongoing because life is always changing. That means our awakening continues to evolve and change too.

Oscillating Through Awakening

This experience of awakeness is beautiful and empowering. When you feel this connection and okayness you will know, "I showed up in my wholeness, I was able to speak my truth. I was able to listen, I was able to open into a new conversation."

But you will also have moments where you're triggered, and you fall back into your old patterning. When that happens, you might feel, "I've gone backwards in my awakening. Here I am showing up in all my old habits."

This, too, is an important part of the journey of awakening. You bring new awareness to see and feel your old habits—this is how they begin to shift. Awareness is a precursor for change. Little by little, all the old, outdated parts of yourself begin to be updated and integrated into new levels of your awake wholeness, even as you oscillate back and forth feeling awake in one moment and so lost in your own stuff in another moment.

This oscillation is a natural part of awakening. Sometimes you open into some new realizations and new capacities, only to quickly fall back into the edges of the places inside that are not awake. That's normal and natural. Awakening doesn't hit every part of us simultaneously. It gives us access to the field, and through the field, we start to touch the places in us that aren't yet awake and bring them into awareness. These parts of the self come forth only when they are ready to be integrated back into wholeness.

When you experience a setback—the kind of day when you don't want to get out of bed, or when you fall into an old pattern you can't shake—try to bring some love and compassion to yourself. Get some support from friends or loved ones. Remind yourself that this is part of the experience. This, too, is part of your wholeness.

Many people think, "Oh, when I awake, I'm going to be like Mother Teresa." No, you're going to wake up and be like you! Your awakening is not about being perfect—it's about being more of yourself. It's about slowly expanding into the wholeness of your being. The oscillations along the way allow you to grow gradually into your wholeness, so your system has time to adjust.

Oscillations are part of the gentle nature of the universe. Change occurs little by little so that we can continue to maintain our established relationships. We feel more awake and less awake, and that allows us to bring more attention, love, and care to those less awake parts of ourselves, so they can grow up and integrate into the wholeness of our being. It's a beautiful reclamation.

On our journey of awakening, we begin to identify more as Fundamental Consciousness. Sourcing our lives from Fundamental Consciousness allows us to mature into greater levels of adult development. It also allows us to show up in life in more powerful and courageous ways. Finally, as we continue on our awakening journey, we also have the confidence and intention to clean up unfinished aspects of our past with greater ease.

Seeing the Gift of Your Awakening

Living an awake life has many benefits. It allows you to more intimately deepen into your relationships. Your relationships with family, friends, coworkers, the earth, and the cosmos itself are all touched. When you realize yourself as Fundamental Consciousness, you're living with this great superpower of connectivity and intimacy, moment to moment, as it unfolds in your everyday life.

You become a transmitter of the awakening that you're living. It's like you're activating a new way of being human, and other people feel it and sense it. This shift impacts those closest to you most, because they're interacting with you the most, but it also ripples out into the world.

You are also likely to connect more with your purpose and passions. A lot of people I work with come into awakening and say, "I want to find my purpose in life. I feel unsatisfied at my job, or I've already raised my children and now I'm ready to reenter life in the workplace. But I don't know what I'm here to do. What's my purpose?"

They expect to find their purpose at the start of their awakening journey. But often, finding your deeper purpose in life, how you really contribute your gifts and talents to the world, comes as a byproduct of waking up to know who you are, and it unfolds in a surprising way as you walk your awakening in life.

Every day, you start to bring more of yourself forward, discovering more of your wholeness. You find new things that you love—for example, music or poetry.

One client who was in the world of financial planning discovered that she had an interest in music. She continued to work in her financial industry, but she took up playing and performing crystal singing bowls as a passion. She now shares that gift and talent with the world, and finds great pleasure in it. And at work, she can show up for her clients in a different way because she is content, peaceful, and awakened.

Gifts of awakening don't always relate to work, although a lot of times, people do find deeper fulfillment in their work. It's also common to wake up and find more of an orientation to a life of service, however that manifests for you. That's because you realize you *are* life. You are one essence that permeates all life. That brings with it a natural inclination to serve creation. This is done not from sacrifice, but as a natural expression of joy—bringing forth the essence of who you are and what delights and inspires you.

For me, the awakened expression of my gifts and talents was to become a spiritual guide for others to the path of embodied awakening. While I had already served many groups prior to my awakening, once I had my awakening, I surrendered to my deeper path of guiding groups of individuals through their awakened journeys. This brought me a greater joy than I had ever experienced before. I felt a greater sense of fulfillment, knowingness, and purpose on earth.

I have seen over and over that once people know who they are, they each find different ways of fulfillment, and they really want to live as a full expression of that.

Becoming One with Creation

As people become more whole within themselves, they embrace the different parts of themselves. One of the greatest gifts of that acceptance is the understanding that we are one with all creation.

Remember Taylor, who I talked about in the last chapter? She told me that she felt like there was plexiglass between her and the rest of the world. After awakening, she told me, "I started to include all the parts of me, even the ones I used to shun that were not perfect, that felt flawed. They all got to have a voice in my wholeness. My awakening continues to deepen all the time, but I finally feel comfortable in my own skin."

Like Taylor, we begin to see that all the parts of us are valid and worthwhile. We become one with ourselves.

That inner realization leads to a reciprocity and a recognition of the seamless connection to the outer world. We see that we are one with all of life, what some people call oneness of creation. There's a felt sense of the connectedness to the earth, to the sky, to the plants, the ocean, and to other people, the ones we like and the ones we don't like. This oneness builds in equal measure internally and externally, each awareness supporting and growing the other.

Before awakening, as I said before, there's a separateness between what's inside and what's outside, and that creates pressure. Holding yourself separate from everyone and everything takes a toll. It seems safer to be this way, and you've been taught to be this way because everybody else is, but it's exhausting. It's like you've been holding an inflated ball underwater for your whole life.

During the embodied awakening, you experience a relaxation of that foundational pressure. For the first time, the ball is able to float to the surface. In the yogic tradition, we call this release *samadhi*. The pressure collapses between inside and outside, and you experience a seamless connection to all of life.

Embodying the Light

Another gift of awake living is a powerful flow of energy that begins to move through your whole body. As you wake up to the field of Fundamental Consciousness, you notice more vitality or energy.

In the yogic tradition, the body comprises many energy channels, or *nadis*. Nadis are rivers of light—the path energy takes to move freely through your body.

In awake living, we are able to differentiate between the levels of physical, mental, emotional, energetic, and spiritual. But the body has a wholeness, and in that more coherent field of Being, energy and light flow more freely in the body. We also sense a greater capacity to open into a higher frequency of light and energy. Think of a garden hose. Instead of a hose that's tangled and crimped, water can now flow freely through us and into the garden of our lives.

In awakening, some people say the cells of their bodies start to feel like they're humming. These people feel more vibrant and more alive, more engaged with life. Rather than being anxious or overwhelmed by energy, they develop a greater ability to allow a more intense, natural flow of energy and aliveness in the body. They more naturally allow emotions to flow and breathe.

Awakening does not mean that all your troubles are gone. You still may encounter challenges, as discussed in chapter 7. But you're able to meet the challenges with less resistance and greater capacity. With awakening, you have access to the field of Fundamental Consciousness and well-being as your identity. The shift in identity allows you to tenderly embrace all the experiences of your life, so whatever arises can be met with greater flow and ease. Living life becomes a magnificent adventure.

You don't have to grow alone. As discussed already, embodied awakening includes the relationships with people around you. As I explore in the next chapter, it also broadens to include a community, people like you who are engaged in following the path of embodied awakening.

Chapter 11

COMMUNITY

There is almost a sensual longing for communion with others who have a large vision. The immense fulfillment of the friendship between those engaged in furthering the evolution of consciousness has a quality impossible to describe.—Pierre Teilhard De Chardin

Traveling Through Heartbreak

Many people have an aversion to joining groups, because in their past, joining a group often meant they had to give up part of themselves in order to fit in. That was the case for my client, Ruby.

Ruby was an intelligent woman, a lawyer with a PhD. She was going through a messy and emotional divorce, and I invited her to join our spiritual awakening community. At first, she was very hesitant. Previously, she'd experienced groups trying to get her to change and be different to conform, and she was afraid of that happening again.

"Just come one time," I suggested. "I think you'll be really surprised."

She agreed. She came to her first session quietly, watching everything and everyone with big eyes. But as she observed our community, she quickly felt the field of acceptance and validation that we emanated. She saw that we welcomed her exactly as she was, and she let go of her hesitation. She opened up and embraced what the group had to offer, and the change was striking.

Ruby was able to speak difficult truths about the divorce, and the anger and shame she felt over her marriage ending. She was held and supported by the community without them needing to fix or change what she was going through. She found a safe space where her difficult emotions were held in the sacredness of the community.

They honored the difficulty of her journey, and that allowed her to go through it with more confidence and more clarity. She found herself better able to handle those challenges, and she found space within herself to hold her difficult emotions. Through the heartbreaking experience of her divorce, with the support of a strong spiritual community, she relaxed into herself and experienced her own embodied awakening.

As we're growing in our awakening journey, it's helpful to have a field of other awake and awakening beings to support us in the tender new growth of unfolding into life and bringing forth our true authenticity. We're relational beings by nature. We need a community to support us and nourish us into growing in our wholeness so that we can give our gifts to the world.

Releasing the Old Paradigm

Centuries ago, as you may know, awakening was considered a solitary pursuit. People left society and their families in order to pursue spiritual awakening. Buddha famously chose to leave his life as a prince. Jesus spent forty days alone in the desert.

Spiritual teachers and guides were forged in solitude. They were few and far between, and their wisdom was much sought after.

This paradigm of believing we have to awaken alone is still prevalent. But in modern society, a new path has begun to develop. The late Thich Nhat Hanh, a prominent Vietnamese Buddhist monk and teacher, was nominated for the Nobel Peace Prize by Martin Luther King Jr. A peace activist in his war-torn country, he also developed spiritual communities in the West. He famously said, "the next Buddha will be a *sangha*"—a "community of people"—rather than an individual person.

In the old paradigm, one person in a million awakened in order to uplift many others. At this time in history, millions of people have awakened around the world. Those initial awakened beings, like Jesus, Buddha, Moses, and

Anandamayi Ma (to name only a few), were ahead of their time, but spiritual awakening is now available to all of us as the next natural stage of human development. Now, it's so much easier and more enjoyable to awaken with others who are on a similar path and can support and encourage you on your journey.

When you're going through challenges, your mind may shout, "Will I ever get through this?" "I'm doing it wrong," or "I'll never get out of this!" If you're alone, your mind may be all you can hear. But if you're in a supportive group, you have some distance from the voice in your head. You connect with people who have gone through similar experiences and expanded from it. In an awakened group, you share with others who have gone through similar difficult emotions and challenging situations. They can hear you, hold you, and feel you, rather than try to change or fix you.

Their individual journeys also provide hope, promise, and inspiration for what's possible for you. In a group, you spend less time lost, circling in the cul-de-sac of your mind, and more time surrendering to your path of awakening.

Craving Community

Humans are biologically hardwired to be with other humans. To process difficult emotions, we need another well-regulated nervous system to balance our own. Contrary to the beliefs of old, awakening is facilitated and enhanced by being in a community of people who each have a commitment to their spiritual awakening.

Community creates a container of teachings and safety and transmission so that your body and mind can naturally relax into the path of spiritual awakening. When you are held by other people as you go through the challenges of your life, you have more resilience, fortitude, and strength. Not awakening in a vacuum, but being in the relational field with others in a spiritual community becomes the training ground for more evolved relationships.

SPIRITUAL COMMUNITY VS. SOCIAL COMMUNITY

Having a spiritual community is different than having strong relationships with friends or family. If you're relying on your friends to help you through your awakening journey, they may be well-intentioned, but they're often just going to try to quickly solve your problems. If you're sad, they want to cheer you up. Spiritual community, on the other hand, gives you a secure container to go through what you need to go through and be loved and supported all the way through it.

When you don't grow with a community, it makes the journey much more difficult. It's harder to give yourself permission to go to difficult places. After all, if it was easy, you would've done it decades ago. Instead of cooperating with what's happening, you are more likely to fight it and fall into old habitual patterns.

In my earlier stages of spiritual awakening, I didn't have a community. When difficult things came up, I would avoid them entirely. I thought I could transcend my emotions to get to spirituality. Once I found an awakening teacher and an awakening community, everything changed. I got support to feel my feelings and be myself, and I was able to relax into my body and open into my awakening.

When you're on a path of awakening and you find your community of awakened and awakening beings, it provides a transmission, a nourishment that you can feel. The Fundamental Consciousness that the group is holding allows you to be more vulnerable. You can be more real, and in so doing can discover your authenticity.

Often when you're discovering your authenticity, speaking your truth, it's like a tiny sprout of grass coming up for the first time. If you do it around people who are going to attack you, or who will trample unknowingly across you, it kills that new sprout of aliveness. That's why you want to be in a container where you're being tended and cared for in your awakening. A spiritual community provides guidance and support, while also giving you the opportunity to offer support to others. This becomes a means to access new ways of being together.

Relating in Whole-Being Ways

You can take the lessons from your spiritual community into the wider world. That was the case for my client Sven. He was an executive management scientist at a fast-paced biotech company. The company was doubling in sales every year, which created a great deal of pressure for the team.

Sven joined our group at his wife's invitation, so they could do it as a couple. At our group meetings, he learned to move his attention from his head to his heart, so he was able to hear people more at an emotional level. Back at work, he was surprised to find that the skills he cultivated in embodied awakening helped him excel as a leader.

He was astounded by how those skills translated to stronger relationships with his team members. He was able to provide emotionally safe spaces by listening to teammates, as well as share in deeper and more authentic ways with them. His coworkers appreciated the depth of vulnerability and authenticity that he brought. This allowed them to feel more comfortable sharing, and their connection created a deeper atmosphere of trust. They were soon working together as a unified team, connecting for the first time. This supported an overall culture of more creativity, collaboration, and innovation.

By learning to be in a safe, supportive community himself, Sven was able to create that environment for others. For the first time, his team acted as a community.

A spiritual community provides a sacred, powerful space. Your community of people on the awakening path can both hold you in your difficult emotions and celebrate you in your shifts. As mentioned before, when people are alone, they tend to pathologize and be critical about what they're going through. But when they're in a spiritual awakening group, they're held and accepted and loved. It's what your nervous system needs to relax. You don't grow with criticism and shame. But you thrive with love, support, and nourishment.

Another important element of being in an awakening community is that it celebrates our growth. In our modern society, we don't have a mechanism for recognizing and celebrating the spiritual transformations we go through. Our society easily celebrates a new house or a new promotion, but not our spiritual shifts. In earlier eras, communities celebrated personal transformations as milestones.

In an awakened community, you have a place where you are seen, held, and recognized as you progress through your journey of awakening. You no longer have to go through it alone. You are given space to mature and awaken.

Building Communities

How do you find a spiritual community? You may feel lost and alone, but many spiritual guides are available to embrace and guide you on your path.

When I was going through my awakening journey, I would travel to awakening workshops. They were incredible experiences where I would feel so awake, and supported . . . while I was there. But as soon as I came back home, I lost that connection. I ended up feeling even more alone and separate.

I longed for a consistent community, and I decided that if I could not find one, I would create one. I started awakening groups at my yoga studio, because I wanted to build a community, both for myself and for other people who were exploring the awakening journey. I also wanted to share what I was learning about awakening and provide a safe container, because I realized how vital and important that is for our development as human beings, and how lacking it is in the world around us.

Even though the people I was teaching had an incredible diversity of experiences, they welcomed each other into this larger container of holding. They used the skills and mutuality of deep listening and embraced each other. When those communities grew and strengthened, I felt great relief. These groups have shifted and evolved over time, but many of my awakening groups have been going on for several years with the same people sharing and helping each other to feel seen and heard.

When you can find that sense of belonging, you can be more fully yourself. And that doesn't just lead to awakening. It continues to support our highest development and unfoldment as awakened beings in the world. It guides us into the field that interconnects us all, where embodied awakening is no longer a purely individual act.

This shared collective field holds us all inside itself. It provides next-level nourishment and support, whether we are physically together or apart, because the field is everywhere. Within this space we can solve greater problems, because we are in a shared collaborative field with each other and with Fundamental Consciousness itself.

The collective field of Fundamental Consciousness allows for the intelligence of life to inform us, move us, and guide us—not just as individuals, but in collaborative spaces. The body of humanity is awakening. This is our next natural stage, and we're not meant to do it alone. Just as individual cells started coming together over a billion years ago to form multicellular organisms in the ocean, we as conscious individuals are coming together now to form an awakened body of humanity.

Community supports us in growing into the next phases of our awakened lives, so we can share our gifts and light with the world.

Chapter 12

LIVING YOUR AWAKENING

The journey of a thousand miles begins with a single step.—Lao Tsu

Living Your Awakening

We have taken a journey together through these pages. But this book, formed of ink on paper or pixels on a screen, by its nature has to come to an end. Your awakening journey, on the other hand, will continue to unfold.

On a recent afternoon, I rode my bike across town to take a yoga class, and as I traveled along a quiet road with the rush of ocean waves on my left side, I was struck by a sense of deep connection. I felt as one with those pounding waves, with the playful wind that blew sweat off my face, and even with the cars rushing past and the buses weaving around traffic. I was connected to the people walking in ones and twos along the boardwalk, leashes or lattes in hand.

When I arrived at yoga class, I felt like I was downloading light right through my body into the poses I shaped.

I brought the love of all creation into life, moment by moment and breath by breath. I saw how big the world was, and that I was both infinite and seamlessly part of it, and I was thankful for the reminder.

Because as much as I would like to, I don't hold that realization every moment of every day. I didn't just master awakening and then I was done. It's an ongoing evolutionary awakening that continues to bring forth the next level of light, and the next level of life. I cherish my sense of growing wholeness. Every day my relationships continue to grow, and my teachings continue to deepen on an eternal unfolding journey

Claiming Ownership of Yourself

Embodied awakening is a daily experience. The practices of listening to and honoring your entire being—emotionally, spiritually, energetically, and physically—unfold more naturally every day. You show up authentically in your relationships and in every conversation. You honor your limits and freedoms, continuing to explore your daily activities and opening to the frequencies of divinity and light. As I continue to teach and guide others, I live my awakening as an outpouring of divinity in the midst of daily life.

Once you have awakened to who you really are, you'll experience next levels of integration into ever-expanding levels of wholeness. Whether you're just beginning your awakening path or you're a seasoned explorer, you can grow in seamless experiences of connection. And you'll find others who have experienced that in an awakened community. You will find and fulfill the wholeness of your humanity and learn to be present to life in Fundamental Consciousness.

With the natural okayness of embodied awakening, you won't be dependent on external factors to feel well-being and security. You will feel secure because you know who you are and you're resourcing off Fundamental Consciousness. You will be able to fully embrace the sacredness of life.

The longing that you have, the intuition that there's something more to life, more to who you are, is a natural part of your evolution. It means that you're ready to take the next step. The universe is inviting you to trust—trust the impulse to follow that longing to awaken to who you are. Trust the challenges you're going through in your life right now. Your everyday life is the sacred ground of your divine awakening journey.

You are a divine human being, and this is your birthright. The love of creation lives in you, as you. Your awakening journey allows you to know and feel that love in yourself and in your life. It's the kind of transformation that changes everything, and you are ready for it.

Say yes to your call of awakening.

ABOUT THE AUTHOR

Geri Portnoy, MA, E-RYT 500, is a dedicated spiritual awakening guide, experienced yoga teacher, and Somatic Experiencing® Practitioner in training. With a passion for supporting and catalyzing humanity's awakening, Geri brings over 25 years of experience in helping people achieve greater health  and well-being. She holds a master's degree in International Peace Studies from the University of Notre Dame, a bachelor's degree in Biology, and a certificate in the Biology of Trauma® at the professional level.

To learn more about my courses and membership programs—and to receive updates, resources, and exclusive content—join my email list at www.geriportnoy.com

www.ingramcontent.com/pod-product-compliance
Lightning Source LLC
Chambersburg PA
CBHW050738150726

48196CB00003B/259